Kenmore

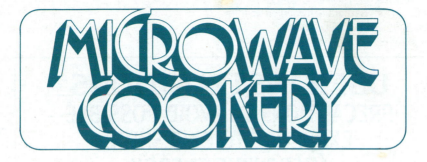

MICROWAVE COOKERY

SEARS

B

BENJAMIN

Home Economics Director: Virginia Peterson
Test Kitchen Supervisor: LuAnne Dugan
Senior Home Economists: Thelma Pressman, Betty Sullivan, Mary Jo Hogue
Managing Editor: Virginia Schomp
Editorial Coordinator: Terry Firkins
Editorial Assistants: Laurie Marzahl, Annemarie Erena, Glen Gilchrist
Project Manager: David P. Stefani
Creative Director: Thomas C. Brecklin
Graphic Artist: Barbara Schwoegler-Boehler
Typography: A-Line, Milwaukee
Photography: Teri Sandison, Los Angeles

USER INSTRUCTIONS
PRECAUTIONS TO AVOID POSSIBLE EXPOSURE TO EXCESSIVE MICROWAVE ENERGY

(a) DO NOT ATTEMPT to operate this oven with the door open since open-door operation can result in harmful exposure to microwave energy. It is important not to defeat or tamper with the safety interlocks.

(b) DO NOT PLACE any object between the oven front face and the door or allow soil or cleaner residue to accumulate on sealing surfaces.

(c) DO NOT OPERATE the oven if it is damaged. It is particularly important that the oven door close properly and that there is no damage to the:
> (1) DOOR (bent)
> (2) HINGES AND LATCHES (broken or loosened)
> (3) DOOR SEALS AND SEALING SURFACES

(d) THE OVEN SHOULD NOT BE ADJUSTED OR REPAIRED BY ANYONE EXCEPT PROPERLY QUALIFIED SERVICE PERSONNEL.

Library of Congress Catalog Card Number: 85-63892
ISBN: 0-87502-182-4
Published by The Benjamin Company, Inc.
One Westchester Plaza
Elmsford, New York 10523
Printed in Singapore
10 9 8
13717

Table of Contents

1. How Does It Work?   4
   An explanation of microwave cooking.

2. What It Does Best   6
   Just a hint to the wonderful quality of microwave cooking.

3. Cooking Techniques and Cookware   8
   What you need to know to understand timing, select cookware, and use your oven efficiently.

4. Getting to Know Your Oven   20
   An explanation of typical oven features and uses.

5. Let's Use the Oven   24
   A step-by-step approach to your first breakfast.

6. On Your Own   26
   Converting conventional recipes and other tips.

7. Defrosting   29
   A guide to quick microwave thawing.

8. Starters and Snacks   37
   An array of after-school, TV-time, or "company's coming" appetizers, snacks, and drinks.

9. Souper Duper Sandwiches   49
   Homemade soups and wonderful, hearty sandwiches.

10. A La Carte   65
    Special vegetable, potato, egg, and cheese dishes that can stand on their own or complement your entrée.

11. One-Dish Dinners   87
    Great budget- and time-savers.

12. Budget-Wise Meat   99
    Recipes that provide a cost-conscious approach to beef, pork, veal, and lamb recipes.

13. Poultry Platters   115
    Chicken, duck, and turkey dress for dinner.

14. Seafood Sampler   129
    Fish and shellfish recipes that are truly a pleasure.

15. Home Baked Goodness   143
    Special cakes, breads, and pies bring back the aroma of yesterday with microwave quickness.

16. Special Treats   159
    Savory sauces, cookies, candies, and fruit.

17. Index   170

HOW DOES IT WORK?

Congratulations! You have selected an exciting cooking appliance that can help you prepare delicious meals in minutes. We will do our part by showing you the way it works, why it works that way, what it can do, and how to quickly become an accomplished microwave cook. What you must do is take time, as with any new appliance, to read the instructions carefully.

A COOKING SCHOOL

These illustrated introductory chapters are designed to be a cooking school in book form. There is nothing complicated about using a microwave oven; all you need is a little understanding of its special qualities and how it responds to food.

To install your microwave oven, follow the Use and Care Manual's directions. You will be pleased to learn your microwave requires little maintenance. Unlike a conventional oven, which generates heat in the oven cavity, there is no heat in the microwave, so food and grease cannot bake on. Just a simple wiping is all your oven needs to keep it clean.

CONVENTIONAL COOKING VS. MICROWAVE

In conventional top-of-the-range cooking by gas or electricity, food cooks by heat applied to the bottom of the pan. In a conventional oven, hot air first heats the oven cavity, then the food. In microwave cooking, no heat source is employed; instead, microwaves are directed to the food. This simple technology eliminates wasted energy. The energy is used only to cook the food, not to heat the air first. Inside the microwave is a magnetron vacuum tube that converts ordinary electric current to high-frequency microwaves.

As in radio and TV sets, these microwaves are designed to perform at a microwave frequency assigned by the FCC (Federal Communications Commission). In the oven, a stirrer-fan helps distribute the microwaves evenly throughout the oven. Microwaves are either reflected, passed through, or absorbed, depending upon the material contacted. Metal reflects microwaves; glass, pottery, paper, and most plastics allow the waves to pass through; and, finally, food absorbs microwaves. The absorbed microwaves cause molecules in the food to vibrate rapidly against each other, producing friction and creating heat. This process is somewhat like the way heat is generated when you rub your hands together. Cooking begins from the outside layer of the food and, by conduction, the interior of food cooks, just as it does in a conven-

Microwaves bounce off oven walls and are absorbed by food. The air in the oven remains cool.

tional oven. It just does it faster. Because cooking containers used in the microwave oven do not absorb microwave energy, they do not become hot unless the heat of the food itself eventually warms the dish. Depending upon the food and the design of the dish, there may be times, however, when you will need to use potholders. The see-through metal screen in the door reflects the microwaves, yet enables you to observe the food as it cooks. Opening the microwave oven door turns the unit off automatically, so you can stir, turn, or check doneness with ease. The removable glass tray helps to elevate the food for even cooking. And all of this with the bonus of an easy-to-clean, cool cavity.

Before we go to cooking school, the next chapter shows us just a few of the ways it will be an enjoyable and tasty education.

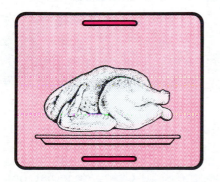

Conventional oven cooks by hot air.

WHAT IT DOES BEST

You can cook just about anything in the microwave oven, but some food is so especially good when done the microwave way that we want to show several of them to you. Let's take a look.

□ *Roast beef* is juicy and rare, with less shrinkage than in the conventional oven. □ *Vegetables* are at their best. Flavor and color are preserved and potatoes are fluffy. □ You'll want *scrambled eggs and bacon* for breakfast, lunch, and supper! Eggs are fluffier than in conventional cooking, and bacon cooks without turning or mess. □ *Cakes* are moist, rich and high. □ *Casseroles* cook without sticking and reheat with no trouble at all.

☐ *Candy* and *bar cookies* are particular favorites for microwave cooks because they are so easy and so good. Try this Dry-Roasted Peanut Brittle (page 163) or the zesty Lemon Bars (page 168) and see for yourself. ☐ The microwave can't be beat for reheating *leftover platters, rolls, and bread* so quickly they are truly perfect.

☐ Explore the pleasures of cooking *seafood* in your microwave oven. Fish fillets and steaks are moist and tender, their natural juices enhancing their delicate flavor. ☐ There s no equal to a *bowl of soup* or a *cup of coffee* served directly from the oven. ☐ *Melt butter (or chocolate)* in seconds and save the mess of burned pans or double boilers.

Now let's look at what you need to know to start cooking.

COOKING TECHNIQUES AND COOKWARE

In this chapter you will find everything you need to know to make microwave cooking easy, efficient, and pleasurable. Once you know the principles, the techniques will become second nature. Read this basic information with its accompanying illustrations carefully. Here you will learn why some foods cook faster than others, what you should know about timing and temperature, which cooking utensils are appropriate, how to cook most efficiently, and much more.

Because of the unique qualities of microwave energy, microwave cooking uses certain terms and methods that are different from those of conventional cooking. For example, in microwave cooking, many foods complete their cooking during *standing time*, after being removed from the oven. In addition, how food is arranged in the cooking dish is important to its being cooked evenly throughout.

ABOUT TIMING

Time is an important element in microwave cooking. But isn't that statement true for all cooking? You, the cook, have to be the judge, as you consider your family's preferences and use your own instincts. Be aware that even though the microwave oven is a superb product of computer technology, it is no more or less precise than any conventional cooking system. Nevertheless, because of the speed with which most food is cooked, timing is more crucial in microwave cooking than in conventional cooking. When you consider that a cooking task requiring one hour in a conventional oven generally needs only one-quarter to one-third, or less, of that time in a microwave oven, you can understand why, in microwave cooking, one minute can be the difference between overcooked or undercooked food.

For that reason, most microwave recipes recommend probable minimum-maximum cooking times, as in "Cook on HI 4 to 5 minutes." This direction is often assisted by a phrase such as "or until tender." As you become familiar with your oven you will recognize when to begin to check for doneness. Remember that it is better to under-cook and add more cooking time than to overcook — then it's too late.

Cooking times might be precise if a way could be found to guarantee that all food would be exactly the same each time we cook it; if the utility company would guarantee not to alter our source of power (there are frequent changes in the voltage levels reaching our homes); and if the size, form, and content of food would be consistently the same. The fact is that one potato or one steak varies from another in density, moisture or fat content, shape, weight, and temperature. This is true of all food. The cook must be ready to adjust to the changes, to be flexible and observant. This discussion really comes down to the fact that you, not the microwave oven, are the cook. The oven can't make judgments, so you must. The recipes in this book have all been meticulously kitchen tested by expert home economists. You will find that the ranges of cooking times suggested are exact. As in all fine cooking, however, microwave cooking needs and benefits from a personal touch.

CHARACTERISTICS THAT AFFECT TIMING

Many characteristics of food, such as quantity, shape, density, and starting temperature, affect timing. Understanding them will help you become a skilled and successful microwave cook.

Quantity

The larger the volume of food there is, the more time is needed to cook it. For example, one potato may cook in 4 to 6 minutes, but 2 potatoes take about one and a half times as long. If the quantity in a recipe is changed, be sure to make an adjustment in timing. When increasing a recipe, increase the amount of cooking time. Here is a general rule to follow: When doubling a recipe, increase the cooking time approximately 50 percent. When cutting a recipe in half, reduce the time by approximately 40 percent.

Density

Dense food such as potatoes, roast beef, and carrots takes longer to cook than porous food, such as cakes, ground beef, and apples,

Irregularly-shaped food requires special arrangement (above). Moist food cooks faster than dry (above left). Food areas close to the oven top are shielded during cooking (left).

because it takes the microwaves longer to penetrate the denser texture. For example, a 2-pound roast will take longer than a 2-pound meat loaf.

Height

As in conventional cooking, areas that are closer to the energy source cook faster. In most microwave ovens, the energy source is at the top of the oven. Food close to the top may require shielding with pieces of aluminum foil or turning over for even cooking.

Shape and Size

Thin food cooks faster than thick food; thin sections faster than thick. Small pieces also cook faster than large pieces. For even cooking, place thick pieces toward the outside of the dish, since the outside areas cook faster than the inside areas. For best results, try to cook pieces of similar size and shape together.

Moisture Content

Moist food cooks faster than dry food because microwave energy is easily absorbed by the moisture within the food. For example, 1 cup of sliced zucchini will cook faster than 1 cup of carrots because of the higher water content in the zucchini. In fact, the amount of free moisture within a food helps determine how rapidly it cooks.

Sugar and Fat Content

Food high in sugar and fat heats more quickly than items low in these ingredients because microwave energy is attracted by sugar and fat. For example, the fruit or cheese filling of a sweet roll will heat faster and be hotter than the roll itself, since sugar and fat reach higher temperatures than food low in sugar or fat content.

Delicate Ingredients

This term is used to refer to food, such as mayonnaise, cheese, eggs, cream, dairy sour cream, etc., that cooks so quickly in the microwave oven that it can overcook and toughen, separate, or curdle. Other food, such as snails, oysters, and chicken livers, may "pop." For this reason, a lower power setting is often recommended for proper cooking. However, when these ingredients are mixed with other food, as in a casserole, stew, or soup, you may use a higher power setting, because volume automatically slows down the cooking.

Starting Temperature

As in conventional cooking, the temperature at which food is placed in the microwave oven affects the length of cooking time. More time is needed to cook food just out of the refrigerator than food at room temperature. For example, it takes longer to heat frozen green beans than canned green beans. Also, hot tap water will start boiling sooner than cold. Recipes in this book start with food at its normal storage temperature.

ABOUT UTENSILS

A wide variety of cookware and cooking implements can be used in the microwave oven. In order to indicate an item made of material that is safe and recommended for microwave cooking, we have created a new term, *microproof.* The Materials Checklist and Guide to Microproof Cookware on the following pages will aid you in selecting the appropriate microproof utensil. Except for metal, most materials are microproof for at least a limited amount of cooking time. But unless specifically approved, items made of metal, even partially, are never to be used in the microwave oven, because they reflect microwaves, preventing them from passing through the cooking utensil into the food. In addition, metal that touches the oven sides will cause sparks, a static charge, known as arcing. Arcing is not harmful to you, though it will deface the oven. Metal twist ties or dishes or cups with gold or silver trim should not be used. See the Materials Checklist for those approved types of metal, such as pieces of aluminum foil used as a shield over certain areas of food to prevent overcooking, or metal clips attached to frozen turkey.

When selecting a new piece of cookware, first check the manufacturer's directions. Also review the Materials Checklist and the Guide to Microproof Cookware. If you are still in doubt, try this test: Pour a cup of water into a glass measure and place it in the oven next to the container or dish to be tested. Cook on HI 1 minute. If the new dish feels hot, don't use it — it is absorbing microwave energy. If it feels warm, the dish may only be used for warming food. If it remains at room temperature, it is *microproof.*

The rapid growth of microwave cooking has created many new products for use in the microwave oven. Among these are microproof replacements for cookware formerly available only in metal. You'll find a wide variety at your store — cake, bundt, and muffin pans, roasting racks, etc. When you add these to traditional microproof cookware and the array of microproof plastic and paper products, you'll find that microwave cooking enables you to select from many more kinds of cookware than are available for conventional cooking.

Selecting Containers

Containers should accommodate the food being cooked. And you must make sure that they fit in your oven. For best results, try to use the particular size or shape of dish cited in a recipe. Varying the container size or shape may change cooking time.

Whenever possible use round or oval dishes. Square corners in cookware receive a higher concentration of energy than the rest of the dish, so food in the corners tends to overcook. Some cake and loaf recipes call for ring molds or bundt pans to facilitate more even cooking. This is because the center area in a round or oval dish generally cooks more slowly than the outside. Round cookware with a small glass inserted open end up in the center also eliminates undercooked centers.

A 2-quart casserole called for in a recipe refers to a bowl-shaped cooking utensil. A 12 × 7-inch or a 9-inch round baking dish refers to a shallow cooking dish. In the case of puddings, sauces, and candies, fairly large containers are specified to prevent boiling over.

Materials Checklist

☐ CHINA, POTTERY: Ideal for microwave use. However, if they have metallic trim or glaze, they are not microproof and should not be used.

☐ GLASS: An excellent microwave cooking material. Especially useful for baking pies to check doneness of pie shells through the bottom. Since ovenproof glass is always safe, "microproof" is not mentioned in any recipe where a glass item is specified.

☐ METALS: *Not* suitable except as follows:

Small strips of aluminum foil can be used to cover areas on large pieces of meat or poultry that defrost or cook more rapidly than the rest of the piece — for example, a roast with jagged areas or thin ends, or the wing or breastbone of poultry. This method is known as *shielding* in microwave cooking.

Shallow aluminum frozen TV dinner trays with foil covers removed can be heated, provided that the trays do not exceed ¾-inch depth. However, TV dinners heat much faster if you "pop" the blocks of food out and place them on microproof plates.

Frozen poultry containing metal clamps may be defrosted in the microwave oven without removing the clamps. Remove the clamps after defrosting.

Trays, foil or metal items must be at least 1 inch from oven walls.

☐ PAPER: Approved for short-term cooking and for reheating. White paper towels, waxed paper, and parchment are suitable coverings. Extended use may cause the paper to burn. Must not be foil-lined.

☐ PLASTICS: Excellent products have been designed for microwave use. Use plastics marked for microwave use and follow the directions of the manufacturer. Plastics that melt from the heat of the food should not be used.

☐ PLASTIC COOKING POUCHES: Can be used. Slit the pouch so steam can escape.

☐ STRAW AND WOOD: Can be used for quick warming. Be certain no metal is used on the straw or wood items.

Browning Dishes

A browning dish is used to sear, grill, fry, or brown food. It is made to absorb microwave energy. A special coating on the bottom of the dish becomes very hot when preheated in the microwave oven. Follow the manufacturer's instructions for use and care and for the length of time to preheat the dish.

After the dish is preheated,

vegetable oil or butter may be added to enhance the browning and prevent food from sticking. After the food is placed on the preheated browning dish, the dish is returned to the oven, where the microwaves are attracted to the food rather than to the dish. The hot surface of the dish browns the food. The food can be turned over to brown the other side. The longer you wait to turn the food, the less browning occurs, since the dish cools off rapidly. You may need to drain the dish, wipe it out, and preheat it again. Since the browning dish becomes very hot, be sure to use potholders.

Familiar items, such as muffin pans and molds, are available in microproof material. Other items, such as bacon racks and browning dishes, have been developed for microwave cooking (above). All kinds of paper products and many plastic ones make microwave cooking easy (above left). A wide variety of glass, ceramic, and wood products are perfect for microwave use (left).

A GUIDE TO MICROPROOF COOKWARE

ITEM	GOOD USE	GENERAL NOTES
China plates, cups	Heating dinners and drinks.	No metal trim.
Cooking pouches (plastic)	Cooking meat, vegetables, rice, other frozen food.	Slit pouch so steam can escape.
Corelle®	Heating dinners, soups, drinks.	Closed-handle cups should not be used.
Corning Ware® or Pyrex casseroles	Cooking main dishes, vegetables, desserts.	No metal trim.
Microwave browning dishes or grills	Searing, grilling, and frying small meat items; grilling sandwiches; frying eggs.	These utensils are specially made to absorb microwaves and preheat to high temperatures. They brown food that otherwise would not brown in a microwave oven.
Microwave roasting racks	Cooking roasts and chickens, squash and potatoes.	Special racks are available for cooking bacon.
Oven film and cooking bags	Cooking roasts or stews.	Substitute string for metal twist ties. Bag itself will not cause tenderizing. Do not use film with foil edges.
Paper plates, cups, napkins	Heating hot dogs, drinks, rolls, appetizers, sandwiches.	Absorbs moisture from baked goods and freshens them. Paper plates and cups with wax coatings should not be used.
Plastic wrap	Covering dishes.	Fold back edge to ventilate, allowing steam to escape.
Pottery and earthenware plates, mugs, etc.	Heating dinners, soups, drinks.	Some pottery has a metallic glaze. To check, use dish test (page 12).
Soft plastics, sherbet cartons	Reheating leftovers.	Use for very short reheating periods.
Thermometers	Measuring temperature of meat, poultry, and candy.	Use only special microwave thermometers in microwave oven.
TV dinner trays (aluminum)	Frozen dinners or homemade dinners.	No deeper than ¾ inch. Food will receive heat from top surface only. Foil covering food must be removed.
Waxed paper	Covering casseroles. Use as a tent.	Prevents splattering. Helps contain heat where a tight seal is not required. Food temperature may cause some melting.
Wooden spoons, wooden skewers, straw baskets	Stirring puddings and sauces; for shish kabobs, appetizers, warming breads.	Can withstand microwaves for short cooking periods. Be sure no metal fittings on wood or straw.

ABOUT METHODS

The evenness and speed of micro-wave cooking are affected not only by the characteristics of food but also by certain cooking meth-ods. Some of these techniques are used in conventional cooking as well, but they are particularly important with microwave cook-ing. Explanations of many other important variables are included here, too.

Microwave arrangement methods create unique cook-and-serve opportunities. The cauliflower and broccoli dish is cooked with ¼ cup water, covered, for 9 minutes on HI.

Arrangement

The way food is arranged in the dish and in the oven enhances even cooking and speeds defrost-ing and cooking food. The micro-waves penetrate the outer por-tion of food first; therefore, food should be arranged so that the denser, thicker areas are near the dish edge, and the thinner, more porous areas are near the center. For example, when cooking broc-coli, split the heavy stalks to expose more area, then overlap with flowerets. Poultry parts are arranged like the spokes of a wheel, with the bony end toward the center. This gives even den-sity to the food and provides even cooking. Place shrimp in a ring with the tails toward the cen-ter. Food such as cupcakes and potatoes should be arranged in a circle, rather than in rows.

Turning Over

As in conventional cooking, some food, such as large roasts, whole poultry, hams, or hamburgers, may require turning over to brown each side and to promote even heating. Any food seared on the browning dish should be turned over. During the defrosting process in the microwave oven, it is often necessary to turn food.

Rotating

Some food, such as pies and cakes, that cannot be stirred, turned over, or rearranged, calls for turning the cooking dish one-quarter turn to allow for even distribution of the microwave energy. Rotate only if the baked food is not cooking or rising evenly. Most food does not need to be rotated.

Turning over (above), rotating (above left), and stirring (left) assist in even cooking.

Stirring

Less stirring is required in microwave than in conventional cooking. When necessary, stir from the outside to the center, since the outside heats faster than the center portion. Stirring blends the flavors and promotes even heating. Stir only as directed in the recipes. Constant stirring is never required in microwave cooking.

Rearranging

Sometimes food that cannot be stirred needs repositioning in the cooking utensil to allow even heating. When rearranging food, move the center food to the outside of the dish and the outer food toward the center.

Piercing

It is essential to pierce the skin or membrane of certain food, such as egg yolks, potatoes, liver, eggplant, and squash. Because they retain moisture during cooking, they must be pierced to prevent bursting and to allow steam to escape. A toothpick may be used for egg yolks; a fork is best for potatoes. Pierce squash deeply with meat fork in 8 or 9 places.

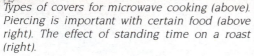

Types of covers for microwave cooking (above). Piercing is important with certain food (above right). The effect of standing time on a roast (right).

Covering

Covers are used to trap steam, prevent dehydration, speed cooking, and help food retain its natural moisture. Suitable tight coverings are microproof casserole tops, glass covers, plastic wraps, oven bags, and microproof plates and saucers. Remove coverings away from your face to prevent steam burns. Paper toweling is especially useful as a light covering to prevent splatter and to absorb moisture. Waxed paper helps retain heat and moisture.

Standing Time

This term refers to the time food needs to complete cooking or thawing, after the microwave time has ended. During standing time, heat continues to be conducted from the outside to the center of the food. After the oven is turned off, food may remain in the oven for standing time or may be placed on a heatproof counter. This procedure is an essential part of food preparation with the microwave oven. Some food, such as roasts, requires standing time to attain the proper internal temperature for rare, medium, or well-done. Casseroles need standing time to allow the heat to spread evenly and to complete reheating or cooking. With cakes, pies, and quiches, standing time permits the center to finish cooking. During the standing time outside the oven, place food on a flat surface, such as a heat-resistant breadboard or counter top, not on a cooling rack.

Shielding

Certain thin or bony areas, such as the wing tips of poultry, the head and tail of fish, or the breastbone of a turkey, cook faster than thicker areas. Covering these parts with small pieces of aluminum foil shields these areas from overcooking, since aluminum foil reflects the microwaves. Be careful not to allow the foil to come closer than 1 inch to the oven walls.

Browning

Some food does not brown in the microwave oven as much as in the conventional oven. Depending upon the fat content, most food will brown in 8 to 10 minutes in the microwave oven. For example, bacon browns in minutes because of its high fat content. For food that cooks too quickly to brown, such as hamburgers, fried eggs, steaks, or cutlets, a special browning dish is available. A longer cooking time or higher fat content will provide more browning. You can also create a browned look by brushing on a browning agent, such as gravy mix, onion soup mix, etc. Cakes, bread, and pie shells do not brown as they do in conventional cooking. Using chocolate, spices, or dark flour helps attain the dark color. Or you can create appealing color by adding frostings or dark spices.

High Altitude Adjustments

As in conventional cooking, microwave cooking at high altitudes requires adjustments in cooking time for leavened products like bread and cake. Other foods may require a slightly longer cooking time to become tender, since water boils at a lower temperature. Usually, for every 3 minutes of microwave cooking time you add 1 minute for the higher altitude. Therefore, a recipe calling for 3 minutes needs 4 minutes and a recipe requiring 6 minutes needs 8 minutes. The wisest way to proceed is to start with the time given in the recipe and then check for doneness before cooking further. Remember: You can always add time, but you can't subtract it once a food is overcooked. Here, again, your judgment is vital.

It may be advisable to consult your local utility for specific information about your area.

GETTING TO KNOW YOUR OVEN

Your microwave oven gives you the ability to select from many power settings, from 0% to 100% (HI). Just as in your conventional oven, these variable power settings let you alter the cooking power to suit the food and thus prepare perfectly cooked dishes. The Guide below lists the main settings and matches each with its familiar cooking term and recommended uses.

Touch Pads

You need only touch the pads on the oven control panel to activate the oven. The beep tone sounds to assure you that your instructions have been entered.

Guide for Power Control Settings

Settings	Suggested Cooking Uses
1	Raising bread dough.
10 (warm)	Softening cream cheese; reheating cream and cheese dips; keeping casseroles and main dishes warm.
20 (low)	Softening chocolate; reheating breads, rolls, pancakes, tacos, tortillas, and French toast; clarifying butter; taking chill out of fruit; reheating small amounts of food.
30 (defrost)	Thawing meat, poultry, and seafood; finish cooking certain casseroles, stews, and some sauces.
40 (braise)	Cooking less tender cuts of meat in liquid and slow-cooking dishes.
50 (simmer)	Cooking stews and soups after bringing to a boil; cooking baked custards and pasta; finish cooking less tender roasts.
60 (bake)	Cooking scrambled eggs.
70 (roast)	Cooking rump roast, ham, veal, and lamb; cooking cheese dishes; cooking eggs, meat loaf, and milk; cooking quick breads and cereal products; cakes.
80 (reheat)	Quickly reheating precooked or prepared foods; heating sandwiches.
90 (sauté)	Quickly cooking onions, celery, and green peppers; reheating meat slices.
HI (max. power)	Cooking tender cuts of meat; cooking poultry, fish, vegetables, and most casseroles; preheating browning dish; boiling water; thickening some sauces; cooking muffins.

Internal Temperature

As in conventional cooking, the most accurate way to gauge doneness is with a food thermometer. However, you *cannot use a conventional meat thermometer* with the microwave oven because it may cause sparks, a static charge known as arcing. Arcing is not harmful to you, though it will deface the oven. Specially designed food thermometers are available for microwave use and some can also be used in your conventional oven. Carefully check the thermometer manufacturer's instructions.

The Guide to Internal Temperatures (page 22) provides a range from 120°F to 180°F. The temperatures in this Guide, however, are 5 to 15 degrees *below* the desired ready-to-carve or eat internal temperature of a food, the reason being that most food rises about 5°F to 15°F during standing time. After 10 minutes of standing time, for example, the temperature of rare beef will reach 140°F, which is its desirable temperature; well done lamb will reach its proper 170°F to 180°F. When using this Guide, then, remember to account

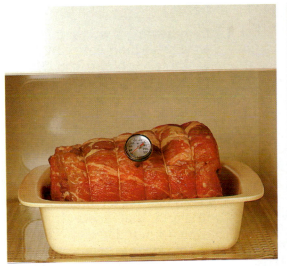

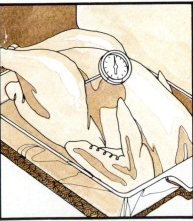

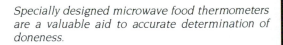
Specially designed microwave food thermometers are a valuable aid to accurate determination of doneness.

for standing time, which is necessary for most food to reach its optimum serving temperature and quality.

Guide to Internal Temperatures	
Suggested Thermometer Readings	
120°	Rare Beef, Precooked Ham
130°	Medium Beef
140°	Fish Steaks and Fillets, Well Done Beef
150°	Vegetables, Hot Drinks, Soups, Casseroles
160°	Meat Loaf
165°	Well Done Lamb, Pork
170°	Poultry Parts, Whole Fish, Well Done Pork
180°	Well Done Whole Poultry

Thermometer Use

As in conventional cooking, the thermometer must be carefully and properly inserted in the food to obtain the best results. Do not allow the thermometer — and, again, remember we are talking about a *special microwave thermometer* — to touch bone or fat. False readings may result. Here are a few tips.

☐ For *roasts*, place the thermometer horizontally in the roast. The tip should be inserted until it reaches the approximate center of the meat.

☐ For *poultry*, place the thermometer between the body and the inner thigh. Avoid bone.

☐ Check *defrosting* food with the thermometer. If the dial drops to a lower temperature or the thermometer cannot be inserted, you know that the food has not reached room temperature or is still frozen.

☐ In *reheating* food, a microwave thermometer can be valuable to obtain exact temperatures for casseroles, soups, and leftovers. (150°F to 170°F are good temperature guides for soups, casseroles, etc.)

☐ In *candy making,* temperature checks are especially helpful. You can obtain microproof candy thermometers, but keep in mind that space in the oven is limited. You can check candy mixture temperatures *outside the oven* with a conventional candy thermometer.

Reheating

One of the major assets of the microwave oven is its efficiency in reheating cooked food. Not only does most food reheat quickly, but it also retains moisture and its just-cooked flavor when properly arranged and covered. If someone is late for dinner, there's no need to fret. Just place a microproof plate containing the cooked food in your oven; in moments, dinner is ready once again. Reheat food in serving dishes or on paper plates and save extra cleanup time. Take-out food, which usually arrives at your home cooled off, can be easily reheated in seconds to its original state in your microwave oven. Leftovers are a treat, too. Follow the tips below to get excellent results when reheating food.

☐ Cook on 80 except when otherwise specified.

☐ To arrange a combination of different foods on a plate, place the dense food, like meat, at the outer edges and the more porous food, like breads, toward the center. Food that cooks most quickly should be placed at the center, with slower cooking food at the edges.

☐ Dense food, such as mashed potatoes and casseroles, cooks more quickly and evenly if a depression is made in the center, or if the food is shaped in a ring.

☐ To retain moisture during reheating, cover food with plastic wrap or a microproof lid. Wrap breads and sandwiches in paper toweling to absorb moisture and prevent sogginess. Use waxed paper to hold heat in and still allow steam to escape.

☐ For quicker and more even heating, spread food out in a shallow container rather than piling it high.

☐ As a general guide to reheating a plate of food, start with 1½ to 2 minutes; then check for doneness. If the plate on which the food is cooked feels warm, the food is probably heated through, for its warmth has heated the plate. Because of the numerous variables in the food to be reheated, i.e., amount, shape, food characteristics, starting temperature, etc., recommended heating times can only be approximate.

LET'S USE THE OVEN

Now it's time for some practical experience using all the features of the microwave oven: first, you'll prepare a quick hot drink, then, a scrambled egg. Let's begin.

Lesson One

A quick pick-me-up

Take your favorite mug or cup; be sure there is no gold or silver trim or metallic glaze. If you are not certain whether your mug is microproof, test it as directed on page 12. Then follow these step-by-step directions.

1. Fill mug or cup with water. Place in the center of the oven. Close the oven door.

2. Touch CLEAR to erase any previous programming. (This is not a necessary step if no previous programming exists).

3. Touch TIME; then touch pads 2-0-0. The oven is set for 2 minutes on HI. (The oven will automatically cook on HI unless a lower setting is entered.)

START

4. Now touch START.

5. The timer will beep when 2 minutes have passed. The oven turns off automatically. Open door.

6. Remove mug. Handle will be

cool enough to hold; cup will be warm from the water. Stir in instant coffee or tea. Enjoy "as is" or go on to prepare a scrambled egg.

Lesson Two

Scrambled Egg

1. Break egg into a microproof bowl or 2-cup glass measure. Add 1 tablespoon milk. Beat with a fork. Add 1 teaspoon butter or margarine.

2. Cover with waxed paper. Place in oven and close door.

3. Touch CLEAR; touch TIME; then touch pads 3 and 0. Touch POWER CONTROL, then pads 6 and 0. The oven is set to cook for 30 seconds on 60.

4. Touch START.

5. After 30 seconds, oven will "beep." Open oven door. Stir egg mixture briskly. Return to oven; close door.

6. Touch TIME; then touch pads 1-0-0. Touch POWER CONTROL, then pads 6 and 0. Oven is set to cook for 1 minute on 60.

7. Touch START. Oven will "beep" and turn off automatically when cooking time ends.

8. Let egg stand 1 minute before serving.

ON YOUR OWN

You will undoubtedly want to cook some of your favorite conventional recipes in the microwave oven. With a little thought and experimenting, you can convert many recipes. Before converting a recipe, study it to determine whether it will adapt well to microwave cooking. Look for a recipe in the book that matches your own recipe most closely. For example, find a recipe with the same amount, type, and form of main ingredient, such as 1 pound ground meat or 2 pounds beef cut in 1-inch pieces, etc. Then compare other ingredients, such as pasta or vegetables. The microwave recipe will probably call for less liquid, because there is so little evaporation in microwave cooking. At the beginning of each recipe chapter hints on adapting recipes are provided. Also use the following guidelines:

☐ Candies, bar cookies, meat loaf, and certain baked goods may not need adjustments in ingredients. For puddings, cakes, sauces, gravies, and some casseroles, liquids should be reduced.

☐ Most converted recipes will require adjustments in cooking time. Although a "rule of thumb" always has exceptions, you can generally assume that most microwave recipes are heated in about one-quarter to one-third of the conventional recipe time. Check for doneness after one-quarter of the time before continuing to cook.

Cooking Casseroles

The microwave oven is exceptionally good for cooking casseroles. Here are some general hints to help you:

☐ Most casseroles can be made ahead of time, refrigerated or frozen, then reheated later.

☐ Many casseroles will require adjustment in the order in which ingredients are added. Cheese toppings, for example, should be added before the last 1 or 2 minutes of cooking. Certain ingredients take longer to cook than others. When converting to microwave, substitute quicker-cooking ingredients, such as precooked rice for long-grain rice and instant onion flakes for chopped onion.

☐ Casseroles are usually covered with plastic wrap or glass lids during cooking.

☐ Allow casseroles to stand 5 to 10 minutes before serving, depending on size. Standing time completes cooking of the casserole center.

☐ You will obtain best results if you make ingredients uniform in size and stir occasionally to distribute heat. If the ingredients are of different sizes, stir more often.

☐ Casseroles containing less tender meat need longer simmering. Those work well when cooked on 30, which gives a slow-cooker effect. Casseroles with delicate ingredients such as cream or cheese sauces often profit from the 30 setting, too.

☐ When used in quick-cooking casseroles, celery, onions, green peppers, and carrots should be sautéed before being added to dish. Rice or noodles should be partially cooked before being added to cooked meat, fish, or poultry.

About Lower Calories

Scattered throughout the book are low-calorie suggestions and low-calorie recipes. They are listed in the index so you can find them when you need them. In general, you can lower calories in many recipes by making substitutions such as these:

☐ Bouillon or water for butter when sautéing or softening vegetables.

☐ Vegetables for potatoes or pasta.

☐ Lean meats for fatty ones.

☐ Whole milk for cream or half-and-half.

☐ Skim milk for whole milk.

☐ Skim milk cheeses like low-fat cottage, ricotta, and mozzarella for creamy, fatty ones.

☐ Natural juices from food mixed with herbs for cream and butter sauces.

☐ Skinless chicken breast for regular cut-up chicken.

☐ Fruit cooked in its natural juices for fruit with sugar added.

By the Way ...

To get the greatest pleasure out of your microwave oven, keep in mind that certain food is best when done by conventional means of cooking. For the following reasons, we don't recommend:

☐ Cooking eggs in the shell, because the light membrane surrounding the yolk collects energy, which then causes a steam build-up that will explode the egg. Don't experiment. It's a mess to clean up!

☐ Deep-fat frying, because the confined environment of the oven is not suited to the handling of the food or oil and is not safe.

☐ Cooking pancakes, because no crust forms. (But the oven is great for reheating pancakes, waffles, and similar items.)

☐ Toasting, because it also requires crust development.

☐ Home canning, because it is impossible to judge exact boiling temperatures inside the jars, and you cannot be sure that the temperature and cooking time are sufficient to prevent contamination.

☐ Cooking chiffon and angel food cakes, because they require steady, dry heat to rise and be tender.

☐ Heating bottles with small necks, like those for syrups and toppings, because they are apt to break from the pressure build-up.

☐ Cooking large items, such as a 25-pound turkey or a dozen baking potatoes, because the space is not adequate and no time is saved.

☐ Cooking true soufflés, because the microwaves tend to make dishes high in egg content a bit rubbery.

About popcorn:

Do not attempt to pop corn in a paper bag, since the corn may dehydrate and overheat, causing the paper bag to catch on fire. Due to the many variables, such as the age of the corn and its moisture content, popping corn in the microwave oven is not recommended. Microwave popping devices are available. While safe to use, they usually do not give results equal to those of conventional popping methods. If the microwave device is used, *carefully follow the instructions provided with the product.*

DEFROSTING

Fish fillets and similar items should be separated halfway through microwave defrosting time with unthawed pieces returned to the oven (left). To defrost ground meat without having portions cook, scrape off thawed pieces with a fork once or twice during defrosting time (above).

One of the most appreciated features of your microwave oven is its ability to defrost food in a fraction of the time required by conventional methods. With today's fast-paced lifestyles, it's not hard to see why microwave defrosting can become a nearly essential part of our lives. We no longer need to be frustrated after a hectic day when faced with the fact that "we forgot" to take something out of the freezer for dinner. Within minutes, an entire meal can be thawed and cooked with this wonderful appliance.

Adding even further convenience, your Kenmore microwave oven has a two-stage programmable memory. Because some food items defrost more evenly if they are separated or turned over during the thawing time, this feature enables you to program an automatic pause when setting the defrosting sequence. Such two-stage defrosting is used for ground beef, fish fillets, roasts, etc. The techniques are described later in this chapter, and complete instructions are provided in the meat, poultry, and seafood chapters.

Keep in mind, though, that microwave defrosting techniques still allow you to give your own special attention to the food, perhaps to speed the defrosting process by use of a cold water bath during the standing time, for example. (Standing time, though often as brief as a few minutes, is necessary to completely thaw all types of food. This method assures that the food does not begin to cook before it is fully defrosted.)

Many of the same principles and techniques that apply to microwave cooking also apply to microwave defrosting. Microwaves are attracted to water or moisture molecules. As soon as the microwaves have thawed a portion of an item, they tend to be more attracted to the increased moisture in the thawed portion. The frozen portion continues to thaw, due in part to the warmth produced in the thawed portion. Special techniques, such as shielding, turning, and rotating, are frequently helpful in preventing the thawed portion from starting to cook before the rest is defrosted. Because of the unknown differences in fat content, density, percentage of bone, etc. in food that the oven can't judge, the defrosting times provided by the defrosting guides throughout this book and in your Use and Care Manual are conservative. Food should be "workable" though it may still be cold or even icy when removed from the oven. Additional standing time may be required to thoroughly defrost some foods.

Helpful Tips

Plastic-wrapped packages from the supermarket meat department may not be wrapped with a plastic wrap recommended for microwave use. Regardless, we recommend removing all meat, poultry, and seafood packaging before defrosting. This is because steam can develop inside the closed package and cause portions to begin cooking.

Metal clips in poultry may be left in until it becomes possible to remove them. They should always be removed before cooking. Metal twists on bags should be replaced with rubber bands.

Vegetables are usually packaged to go right into the microwave for defrosting and heating to serving temperature. It is not necessary to use a defrost power control setting (usually 30) for frozen vegetables. They defrost/reheat on HI.

Poultry wings, legs, and the small or bony ends of meat or fish may need to be covered with pieces of aluminum foil for part of the thawing time to prevent cooking while the remainder thaws.

Large items should be turned and rotated halfway through defrosting time to provide more even thawing.

Do not thaw food wrapped in aluminum or in foil dishes. Traditional TV dinners in foil trays may

Poultry and meat can begin defrosting in their original wrappers; but remove packaging as soon as possible. Fruit and vegetables can be thawed in their packages.

be reheated, if desired, with top foil covering removed. Keep tray 1-inch from oven walls.

The edges will begin cooking if meat, fish, and seafood are completely thawed in the microwave oven. Therefore, food should still be icy in the center when removed from oven. It will finish thawing while standing.

Thin or sliced items, such as fish fillets, meat patties, etc., should be separated as soon as possible. Remove thawed pieces and allow others to continue thawing.

Food textures influence thawing time. Relatively porous foods like cake and bread defrost very quickly and must be checked frequently.

Remove portions of ground meat as soon as thawed. Allow remainder to continue thawing.

Casseroles, saucy foods, vegetables, and soups usually require stirring two or three times during defrosting to redistribute heat. For broth-based soups: start at HI and reduce power to 50 halfway through defrosting time. Stir twice. For stirrable casseroles and thick or cream-based soups: start at 70 and reduce power to 30 halfway through defrosting time. Stir three times.

VOLUME	TIME
1 pint	10 - 15 min.
1 quart	25 - 35 min.
2 quarts	35 - 40 min.
3 quarts	40 - 45 min.
4 quarts	45 - 55 min.

Large items should be turned and rotated approximately halfway through the defrosting time to allow food to thaw more evenly.

Frozen fried foods may be defrosted but will not be crisp when heated in the microwave oven. Of course, new products are introduced every day and we have even seen French fries specially packaged for microwave reheating.

Freezing Tips

It is helpful to freeze in small quantities rather than in one large piece. This will promote more even microwave defrosting.

When freezing casseroles, it's a good idea to insert an empty paper cup in the center so no food is present there. This speeds thawing. Depressing the center of ground meat when freezing also hastens thawing later.

The microwave oven is an excellent appliance to use in preparing vegetables for freezing. A special microwave blanching guide is provided in the vegetables chapter.

LESSON PLAN

To help you become thoroughly familiar with your oven's convenient defrost method and its use, we have provided step-by-step instructions for you. You will soon see how microwave defrosting can transform defrosting from a time-consuming nuisance to a simple preparation step. Let's begin by defrosting 1 pound of ground beef.

1. Unwrap beef and place in a microproof dish or tray to catch drippings. Set dish in the oven on the glass tray.

2. To determine the timing, consult the Guide on page 101. You'll note that 1 pound of ground beef takes between 5 and 6 minutes to defrost. It also calls for turning the beef over and removing any thawed portions. You are now ready to program the oven.

3. Touch CLEAR.

4. Touch TIME. Touch 3-0-0.

5. Touch POWER CONTROL. Touch 3-0.

6. Touch PAUSE. (The oven has been programmed to defrost for 3 minutes at 30% power for the first stage.)

7. Touch TIME. Touch 2-3-0. (We've selected the exact halfway point between 5 and 6 minutes.)

8. Touch POWER CONTROL. Touch 3-0. (The second stage is programmed.)

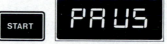

9. Touch START. The oven will begin the first stage and the display window will show the time as the 3 minutes "count down." The oven will stop automatically and "PAUS" will appear in the display window.

10. At the pause, remove thawed portions to a separate dish with a fork, turning beef over and also removing thawed portion from bottom. Return remainder to oven.

NOTE: Meat should still be cold when removed from the oven, and even a bit icy. Defrosting will be completed during the standing time.

11. Touch START. The oven resumes defrosting, and the display window counts down the second stage of 2 minutes 30 seconds. When the time is over, a tone will sound as the oven shuts off automatically. Remove beef.

QUARTERED CHICKEN

Defrost Time: 10 minutes

2 pounds frozen chicken parts

Remove chicken from package and place in microproof baking dish. Place in oven. Defrost on 30, 5 minutes.

Turn parts over and separate. Cover any warm areas with small strips of aluminum foil, keeping foil at least 1 inch away from oven wall. Defrost on 30, 5 minutes.

Let stand 10 to 15 minutes.

GROUND BEEF

Defrost Time: 5½ minutes

1 pound frozen lean ground beef

Remove beef from package and place in shallow microproof baking dish. Place in oven. Defrost on 30, 3 minutes.

Turn over. Remove thawed portions with fork. Defrost on 30, 2½ minutes.

Let stand 5 minutes.

PORK CHOPS

Defrost Time: 12 minutes

2 pounds frozen pork chops, ½-inch thick

Remove chops from package and place in microproof baking dish. Place in oven. Defrost on 30, 6 minutes.

Separate chops. Defrost on 30, 6 minutes.

Let stand 5 to 10 minutes.

ROLLED RIB ROAST

Defrost Time: 24 minutes

1 frozen rolled rib roast (3 pounds)

Remove all wrapping and place roast in microproof baking dish. Place in oven. Defrost on 30, 12 minutes.

Turn roast over. Cover any warm areas with small strips of aluminum foil, keeping foil at least 1 inch away from oven wall. Defrost on 30, 12 minutes.

Let stand 30 to 45 minutes.

SHRIMP

Defrost Time: 4 minutes

1 package (1 pound) frozen shrimp

Remove shrimp from package and arrange in round shallow microproof baking dish with tails toward center of dish. Place in oven. Defrost on 30, 2 minutes.

Rearrange. Defrost on 30, 2 minutes.

Let stand 5 minutes.

FISH FILLETS

Defrost Time: 6 minutes

1 pound frozen fish fillets

Remove fillets from package and place in shallow microproof baking dish. Place in oven. Defrost on 30, 3 minutes.

Turn over. Defrost on 30, 3 minutes.

Let stand 5 minutes. Separate fillets under cold water.

WHOLE FISH

Defrost Time: 6 minutes

1 frozen fish (10 ounces)

Remove fish from package. Place fish in shallow microproof baking dish. Cover head with aluminum foil, keeping foil at least 1 inch away from oven wall. Place in oven. Defrost on 30, 3 minutes.

Turn over. Cover any warm areas with small strips of aluminum foil, keeping foil at least 1 inch away from oven wall. Defrost on 30, 3 minutes.

Let stand 5 minutes.

WHOLE CHICKEN

Defrost Time: 24 minutes

1 frozen broiler-fryer chicken (3 pounds)

Remove chicken from package. Place chicken, breast-side up, in microproof baking dish. Place in oven. Defrost on 30, 12 minutes.

Turn chicken over. Cover any warm areas with small strips of aluminum foil, keeping foil at least 1 inch away from oven wall. Defrost on 30, 12 minutes.

Let stand in cold water 25 to 30 minutes.

STEW BEEF

Defrost Time: 10 minutes

2 pounds frozen beef for stew

Remove beef from package and place in shallow microproof baking dish. Place in oven. Defrost on 30, 5 minutes.

Turn over. Separate beef into pieces. Defrost on 30, 5 minutes.

Let stand 8 to 10 minutes.

LEG OF LAMB

Defrost Time: 25 minutes

1 frozen leg of lamb (5 pounds)

Remove all wrappings and place meat on microproof roasting rack. Place in oven. Defrost on 30, 9 minutes.

Turn meat over. Defrost on 30, 9 minutes.

Turn meat over. Cover any warm areas with small strips of aluminum foil, keeping foil at least 1 inch away from oven wall. Defrost on 30, 7 minutes.

Let stand 15 to 20 minutes.

STARTERS AND SNACKS

Polynesian Meatballs (page 43) and Nacho Rounds (page 46) are arranged in the circular microwave pattern (left). Arrange drinks the same way (above).

Whether you choose to call them tidbits, snacks, or appetizers, they always rate high with the family and guests. The incredible speed of the microwave oven makes all the last-minute hustle and hassle disappear. You can really be part of the party!

Start off a special family meal with Tomato Jalapeño Cheese Dip (page 44) or Olive and Bacon Wraps (page 46). If you want to surprise friends during the next "come-on-over" night, Chicken Wings Canton (page 44) and Mexican Stuffed Mushrooms (page 42) will surely make them wonder where you found the time to fuss.

Hot drinks are in this chapter, too, because they can make any snack a special treat.

And how about those days when the kids drag in from school. Perk up their day with Beef Muffin Toppers (page 39) and a mug of our Spiced Cider (page 42).

Converting Your Recipes

Most of your favorite hot appetizers will adapt well to microwave cooking, except those wrapped in pastry. Pastry requires the hot environment of the conventional oven to become crisp. The recipe for Olive and Bacon Wraps (page 46) is an ideal guide for adapting countless appetizer recipes containing seafood, chicken, vegetable, and fruit combinations. Here are some helpful tips:

☐ Toppings for canapés can be made ahead, but do not place on bread or crackers until just before heating. This assures a crisp base.

☐ Cover appetizers or dips only when the recipe specifies doing so. Use casserole lids, waxed paper, plastic wrap, or paper towels.

☐ Compare your favorite dip recipe with one of the choices here to determine your microwave time.

☐ While the microwave oven is not recommended for baking pastry appetizers, it is perfect for reheating such items.

☐ Appetizers and dips that contain cheese, mayonnaise, and other delicate ingredients are usually heated on 10. A higher setting might cause separation or drying.

REHEATING GUIDE — CONVENIENCE APPETIZERS

Food	Amount	Power Control Setting	Time	Special Notes
Canned meat spread	4 oz.	80	30 - 45 seconds	Transfer to small microproof bowl.
Canned sausages, cocktail sausages	5 oz.	80	1½ - 2 minutes	Place in microproof casserole. Cover with casserole lid.
Cocktail franks, pizza roll	4 servings	70	45 - 60 seconds	Place on paper towels. Roll will not crisp.
Cooked pizza, 10 inches, cut in 8 portions	1 wedge	80	45 - 60 seconds	Place on paper towels or paper plate or leave in uncovered cardboard box, points toward center.
	4 wedges	80	1½ - 2 minutes	
	Whole	70	3¼ - 4 minutes	
Dips, cream	½ cup	10	1½ - 2½ minutes	Cover with plastic wrap.
Eggrolls, Mini Tacos	6 oz. (12)			Follow package directions. Follow package directions.

COOKING GUIDE — HOT DRINKS

Liquid	Power Control Setting	6-ounce Cup	Time (minutes)	8-ounce Cup	Time (minutes)	Special Notes
Water	HI	1 2	1 to 1¼ 1¾ to 2	1 2	1½ to 2 3 to 3¼	For instant coffee, soup, tea, etc.
Milk	70	1 2	2½ 2¾ to 3	1 2	2¾ to 3 3¼ to 3½	For cocoa, etc.
Reheating coffee	HI	1 2	1 to 1½ 2 to 2¼	1 2	1¼ to 1½ 2 to 2½	

Crab-Stuffed Mushrooms ——————— 4 dozen

Total Cooking Time: 6 to 8 minutes

1 **can (6½ ounces) crab, drained**
1 **package (3 ounces) cream cheese, at room temperature**
1 **tablespoon mayonnaise**
2 **teaspoons diced pimiento**
1 **teaspoon prepared mustard**
½ **teaspoon lemon juice**
½ **teaspoon minced onion flakes**
48 **fresh mushroom caps**

Combine all ingredients, except mushrooms, in small mixing bowl; blend well. Fill each mushroom cap with about 1 teaspoon filling. Place 10 to 12 mushrooms, stuffing-side up, in a circle on microproof plate. Cook on HI 1½ to 2 minutes, or until heated through. Repeat with remaining mushrooms.

Beef Muffin Toppers ——————— 2 servings

Total Cooking Time: 1½ minutes

⅓ **cup lean ground beef**
1 **English muffin, split and toasted**
½ **teaspoon garlic powder**
¼ **teaspoon salt**
  Dash freshly ground pepper
¼ **cup shredded Cheddar or 1 slice processed Cheddar cheese, halved**

Divide beef and spread with a knife on muffin halves. Sprinkle garlic powder, salt, and pepper evenly on muffin halves. Place on microproof plate. Cook on HI 1½ minutes. Sprinkle shredded cheese or place ½ slice cheese on each serving. Let stand 1 minute, or until cheese is melted. Serve hot.

Liver Brandy Spread _____ 3 cups
Total Cooking Time: 6 to 7½ minutes

**1 pound chicken livers,
   rinsed and drained**
1 small onion, chopped
½ cup diced celery
¼ cup unsalted butter
1 clove garlic, halved
**Dash freshly ground
   pepper**
2 tablespoons brandy
**1 hard-cooked egg,
   chopped**

Pierce livers with toothpick in several places. Combine livers, onion, celery, butter, garlic, and pepper in 2-quart glass measure. Cover. Cook on HI 6 to 7½ minutes, or until livers lose pinkness, stirring once during cooking time. Allow to stand, covered, 10 minutes. Purée liver mixture and brandy in electric blender or food processor. Pour into serving bowl and sprinkle with chopped egg. Chill for several hours before serving.

Cold Eggplant Appetizer _____ 2 cups
Total Cooking Time: 7½ to 9 minutes

1 eggplant (1 pound)
1 small onion, minced
**½ medium green pepper,
   seeded and minced**
1 clove garlic, minced
1 teaspoon lemon juice
¼ teaspoon salt
**⅛ teaspoon freshly ground
   pepper**
1 cup plain yogurt

Rinse eggplant and place on microwave roasting rack. Pierce skin in several places. Cook on HI 6 to 7 minutes, or until soft. Set aside to cool. Combine onion, green pepper, garlic, and lemon juice in small microproof bowl. Cook on HI 1½ to 2 minutes, or until vegetables are limp. Cut eggplant in half, remove seeds, and scoop pulp into small mixing bowl. Stir in onion mixture, salt, and pepper. Beat until well blended. Stir in yogurt, cover, and chill thoroughly before serving.

Serve with pumpernickel or black bread, party rye or crackers. Cold eggplant is a wonderful low-calorie appetizer. If you serve it with cut-up raw vegetables instead of bread, it is even lower in calories.

Liver Brandy Spread, Crab-Stuffed Mushrooms (page 39) ·➤

Hot Buttered Lemonade _____ 4 servings

Total Cooking Time: 6 to 8 minutes

1 **can (6 ounces) thawed
   frozen lemonade**
3 **cups water**
8 **whole allspice**
8 **whole cloves**
3 **tablespoons rum or
   brandy (optional)**
4 **teaspoons butter or
   margarine**
4 **sticks cinnamon**

Combine lemonade, water, allspice, and cloves in 2-quart glass measure; stir. Cook on HI 6 to 8 minutes, or until hot. Stir in rum. Pour into warm mugs. Top each with 1 teaspoon butter. Place cinnamon stick in each mug as stirrer. Serve hot.

Mexican Stuffed Mushrooms _____ 2 dozen

Total Cooking Time: 5½ to 7 minutes

¼ **pound lean ground beef**
1 **tablespoon taco hot
   sauce**
1 **small tomato, seeded
   and finely diced**
24 **large fresh mushrooms,
   stems removed**
¼ **cup shredded Cheddar
   cheese**

Place ground beef in 1-quart micro-proof casserole; break up with spoon. Cook on HI 2½ to 3 minutes; drain. Add hot sauce and tomato; blend well. Fill each mushroom with about 1 teaspoon filling. Place 10 to 12 mushrooms, stuffing-side up, in circle on microproof plate. Sprinkle with cheese. Cook on HI 1½ to 2 minutes, or until cheese is melted. Repeat with remaining mushrooms. Serve hot.

Spiced Cider _____ 1 quart

Total Cooking Time: 15 minutes

1 **quart apple cider**
¼ **cup firmly packed light
   brown sugar**
½ **teaspoon whole cloves**
½ **teaspoon whole allspice**
1 **cinnamon stick
   Dash salt**

Combine all ingredients in 2-quart microproof casserole. Cook on 50 for 15 minutes, or until hot. Remove spices. Serve hot, garnished with slices of red apple, if desired.

Polynesian Meatballs _____ 48 meatballs

Total Cooking Time: 18 to 19 minutes

2 eggs, slightly beaten
⅓ cup milk
⅓ cup dried bread crumbs
**2 tablespoons instant
    minced onion**
**⅛ teaspoon freshly ground
    pepper**
¼ teaspoon salt
1½ pounds lean ground beef
4 teaspoons cornstarch
½ teaspoon ground ginger
3 tablespoons soy sauce
**1 can (14½ ounces) beef
    broth (1¾ cups)**
¼ cup honey
**1½ teaspoons sherry or
    sweet vermouth**
1 clove garlic, minced

Combine eggs, milk, bread crumbs, onion, pepper, salt, and ground beef in mixing bowl; mix well. Shape mixture into 48 1-inch meatballs. Arrange half of meatballs in double row on round microproof plate. Cover with waxed paper. Cook on HI 5 minutes, or until meatballs are firm. Drain. Cover to keep warm. Repeat with second plate.

Combine cornstarch, ginger, and soy sauce in small bowl; stir to dissolve cornstarch. Combine beef broth, honey, sherry, and garlic in 4-cup glass measure; stir in soy sauce mixture. Cook on HI 8 to 9 minutes, or until thickened, stirring once each minute after 4 minutes. Place meatballs in chafing dish or serving bowl. Pour sauce over meatballs. Serve warm with toothpicks.

Nibblers Bowl _____ 2½ quarts

Total Cooking Time: 7 to 9 minutes

**2 cups small cheese
    crackers**
**2 cups shredded crisp
    wheat squares**
**2 cups shredded crisp corn
    squares**
2 cups thin pretzels
1 cup salted mixed nuts
⅓ cup butter or margarine
½ teaspoon onion salt
¼ teaspoon garlic powder
**1 tablespoon Worcester-
    shire sauce**
**¼ cup grated Parmesan
    cheese**

Combine crackers, wheat and corn squares, pretzels, and nuts in 4-quart microproof mixing bowl; mix lightly; set aside. Place butter in 2-cup glass measure. Cook on HI 1 minute. Stir in onion salt, garlic powder, and Worcestershire. Drizzle over mixture in bowl; stir to coat evenly. Cook on 80 for 6 to 8 minutes, or until mixture begins to toast, stirring twice during cooking time. Sprinkle with Parmesan cheese; stir. Serve warm or at room temperature.

_____

There are many variations of this snack. Make your own substitutions, but follow these instructions and timing.

_____

Chicken Wings Canton ———————— 2 to 4 servings

Total Cooking Time: 12 to 14 minutes

6 chicken wings
¼ cup soy sauce
½ cup fine cracker crumbs
½ teaspoon garlic powder
½ teaspoon paprika
¼ teaspoon ginger
⅛ teaspoon freshly ground pepper

Cut wings in half; discard tips, or save for use in chicken broth. Rinse; pat dry with paper towels. Pour soy sauce into shallow bowl; set aside. In another shallow bowl, combine remaining ingredients. Dip chicken in soy sauce; roll in seasoned crumbs, coating evenly. Arrange chicken wings, skin-side up, in spoke pattern in 9-inch round glass pie plate, placing thickest portions toward outside of plate. Cover with paper towels. Cook on HI 7 minutes. Rotate dish one-quarter turn. Cook on HI 5 to 7 minutes, or until chicken is tender. Serve hot.

Tomato Jalapeño Cheese Dip ———— about 4 cups

Total Cooking Time: 5 to 7 minutes

2 pounds process American cheese, cubed
1 can (1½ ounces) tomatoes and jalapeño peppers, drained
1 can (5.3 ounces) evaporated milk

Combine all ingredients in 2-quart glass measure or microproof bowl. Cook on HI 5 to 7 minutes, or until cheese is melted, stirring once during cooking time. Blend thoroughly with electric mixer. Pour into serving bowl. Serve with corn chips or dipping-style potato chips.

Extra dip can be frozen in plastic containers. To reheat, cook on 50 for 1 minute. Stir and repeat until dipping consistency.

Chicken Wings Canton, Tomato Jalapeño Cheese Dip   ➡

Olive and Bacon Wraps ⎯⎯⎯⎯⎯⎯ 2 dozen

Total Cooking Time: 16 to 18 minutes

12 slices bacon
1 jar (4¾ ounces) large
    stuffed green olives,
    (about 24), drained
2 tablespoons brown
    sugar, divided

Cut bacon slices in half. Wrap half slice of bacon around each olive, securing with toothpick. Arrange half the olives in circle on paper towel-lined microproof plate. Sprinkle with 1 tablespoon of sugar. Cover with paper towel. Cook on HI 6 to 7 minutes. Turn olives over. Cover. Cook on HI 2 minutes, or until bacon is cooked. Let stand 1 minute before serving. Repeat with remaining olives.

Nacho Rounds ⎯⎯⎯⎯⎯⎯⎯ 4 to 6 servings

Total Cooking Time: 5 to 8 minutes

1 package (8 ounces)
    tortilla chips
2 cups shredded Cheddar
    cheese
1 can (4 ounces) diced
    green chilies, drained
1 can (2¼ ounces) chopped
    ripe olives, drained

Arrange chips on two 10-inch microproof serving platters. Cover each with cheese, chilies, and olives. Cook on 70, 1 plate at a time, 2½ to 4 minutes, or until cheese is melted. Repeat with remaining plate.

Shrimp Cream Cheese Dip _____ 2 cups

Total Cooking Time: 2 to 3 minutes

1 **package (8 ounces) cream cheese, quartered**
1 **can (7 ounces) broken shrimp, drained**
2 **tablespoons catsup or chili sauce**
1 **teaspoon instant minced onion**
1 **teaspoon prepared mustard**
1 **teaspoon Worcester- shire sauce**
¼ **teaspoon garlic powder**

Combine all ingredients in 1-quart microproof casserole. Cook on HI 2 to 3 minutes, or until warm, stirring once during cooking time. Stir; serve with crackers or chips.

To reduce calories, substitute low-fat Neufchatel for cream cheese and sub- stitute raw vegetables for crackers or chips. Zucchini rounds are especially nice and can even be topped with the dip, as a spread.

Wine Warmer _____ 8 servings

Total Cooking Time: 7 minutes

⅕ **gallon full-bodied red wine**
3 **teaspoons sugar**
  Orange peel, cut in 2-inch strips
2 **cinnamon sticks**

Combine all ingredients in 2-quart glass measure or microproof bowl. Cook on 50 for 7 minutes. Do not boil. Serve in mugs garnished with an orange slice.

Clam Cheddar Cheese Dip _____ 3 cups

Total Cooking Time: 3 to 4 minutes

1 **can (6½ ounces) minced clams, drained, ¼ cup juice reserved**
2 **cups shredded sharp Cheddar cheese**
1 **package (8 ounces) cream cheese, quartered**
1 **tablespoon Worcestershire sauce**
⅓ **cup minced green pepper**
2 **tablespoons thinly sliced green onion**
¼ **teaspoon hot pepper sauce (optional)**

Combine clams, reserved juice, cheeses, Worcestershire, green pepper, and onion in 1½-quart microproof cas- serole. Stir; cover. Cook on HI 3 to 4 minutes, or until cheese is melted, stirring after 1 minute. Stir until well blended; stir in pepper sauce. Serve at room temperature with vegetables, such as raw celery, cucumbers, zucchini, radishes, and cauliflowerets.

Hot Chocolate Malt _____ 4 servings

Total Cooking Time: 5 to 6 minutes

2 cups milk
¼ cup chocolate syrup
**4 tablespoons instant
      malted milk powder**

Combine all ingredients in 4-cup glass measure. Cook on 70 for 5 to 6 minutes, or until hot, stirring once during cooking time. Serve in warm mugs.

Pizza Topper _____ 1 to 2 servings

Total Cooking Time: 45 to 60 seconds

**1 English muffin, split and
      toasted**
2 tablespoons pizza sauce
6 slices pepperoni
**2 tablespoons shredded
      mozzarella cheese**

Spread each muffin half with pizza sauce. Top each with 3 slices pepperoni and then with cheese. Place halves on microproof plate. Cook on 60 for 45 to 60 seconds, or until cheese is melted. Let stand 2 minutes before serving.

If desired, 2 muffins may be prepared and cooked together. To do so, double ingredients and place muffin halves in circle on microproof plate. Cook on 60 for 1½ to 2 minutes, or until cheese is melted. Let stand 2 minutes before serving.

SOUPER DUPER SANDWICHES

A microproof plate makes a dandy cover for a microproof bowl when preparing soup (right). Microwave browning dishes can enhance the flavor and appearance of hamburgers (above).

Yes, indeed, soup is super when prepared in the microwave oven! You can prepare canned or instant soup right in the serving bowl or mug. But don't you agree that nothing is more reassuring than a steaming bowl of your very own homemade soup? Now, you'll prepare your own more often. Imagine the convenience of cooking in the serving tureen (any large and attractive casserole will do) and then ladling leftover soup from the refrigerator container into a mug for reheating and serving.

No pan to clean!

Sandwiches, too, are so easy and most can be prepared simply on a paper plate.

Best of all, of course, are the marvelous soup and sandwich combinations you can serve for lunch, brunch, or a quick dinner. Here are two of our selections: Manhattan Seafood Chowder (page 56) with Tuna, Tomato, and Cheese (page 64), and Quick Minestrone (page 55) with Super Sandwich (page 62).

Converting Your Recipes

An enormous variety of sandwich combinations can be made in your microwave oven. Sandwiches heat quickly, so be careful not to overcook — the bread can become tough and chewy. Heat breads until warm, not hot, and cheese until it just begins to melt. Let these tips guide you when adapting or creating your own sandwiches.

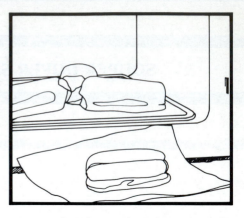

Arrange hot dogs and similar items end-to-end for even heating (above).

☐ The best breads to use for warmed sandwiches are day-old, full-bodied breads such as rye and whole wheat, and breads rich in eggs and shortening, like French or Italian and other white breads.

☐ Heat sandwiches on paper napkins, paper towels, or paper plates to absorb the steam and prevent sogginess. To prevent splattering, you can wrap each sandwich in a paper towel. Remove wrapping immediately after warming. It takes less than 1 minute to heat most sandwiches. Cook on 80.

☐ A few thin slices of meat heat more quickly and taste better than one thick slice. The slower-cooking thick slice often causes bread to overcook before meat is hot.

☐ Moist fillings, such as that in a Sloppy Joe or a barbecued beef sandwich, should generally be heated separately from the rolls, to prevent sogginess.

☐ The browning dish can be used to enhance your grilled cheese or Reuben. Brown the buttered outer side of bread before inserting filling.

Soup converts well and easily to the microwave method. Find a recipe here with the approximate density and volume of the family favorite or the new conventional recipe you want to try. You may have to alter an ingredient or two: for example, dried bean soups, such as split pea and navy bean, do not obtain the best results in microwave cooking. However, canned, precooked beans and packaged dry soup mixes are perfect substitutes. The following tips will help you obtain excellent results with your own recipes.

- ☐ Be careful with milk-based liquids or large quantities, which can boil over quickly. Always select a large enough microproof container to prevent any boiling over, and fill individual cups no more than two-thirds full.
- ☐ Soup is cooked covered. Use microproof casserole lids, waxed paper, or plastic wrap.
- ☐ Cooking time varies with the volume of liquid and density of food in soup.
- ☐ Remember that the microwave's brief cooking time results in less evaporation of liquid than stovetop simmering.
- ☐ Start with one-quarter the time recommended in a conventional recipe and adjust as needed to complete cooking.
- ☐ The temperature of the liquid before heating will make a difference in final heating time. Water cold from the tap or drinks from the refrigerator will take somewhat longer than hot tap water or any liquid at room temperature.
- ☐ You can use a microwave thermometer to reheat soup. Most people prefer 150°F for soup.

COOKING GUIDE — CANNED SOUPS

Soup	Amount	Power Control Setting	Time (minutes)	Special Notes
Broth	10¾ oz.	80	3½ - 4	Use 1½-quart microproof casserole.
Cream-Style	10¾ oz.	80	5 - 6	Use 1½-quart microproof casserole.
Tomato	26 oz.	80	8 - 10	Use 2-quart microproof casserole.
Bean, Pea, or Mushroom	10¾ oz.	70	7 - 8	Use 1½-quart microproof casserole.
Undiluted chunk-style vegetable:	10¾ oz.	80	2½ - 4	Use 1-quart microproof casserole.
	19 oz.	80	5 - 7	Use 1½-quart microproof casserole.

- Add milk or water as directed on can. Stir.
- Stir cream-style soup halfway through cooking time.
- Let stand, covered, 3 minutes before serving.

COOKING GUIDE — QUICK SOUPS

Soup	Number of Envelopes	Power Control Setting	Time (minutes)	Special Notes
Instant soup 1¼-ounce envelope	1	HI	2 - 2½	Use ⅔ cup water in 8-ounce mug.
	2	HI	3 - 3½	Use ⅔ cup water per 8-ounce mug.
	4	HI	6 - 7	Use ⅔ cup water per 8-ounce mug.
Soup mix 2¾-ounce envelope	1	HI	8 - 10	Use 4 cups water in 2-quart microproof casserole.

Eldorado Chili _____ 4 servings

Total Cooking Time: 25 to 29 minutes

1 pound lean ground beef **½ cup minced onion** **½ cup chopped green** **pepper** **1 clove garlic, minced** **1 can (28 ounces)** **tomatoes, broken up** **1 can (15 ounces) kidney** **beans, undrained** **½ cup broken spaghetti** **1½ to 2 tablespoons** **chili powder** **½ teaspoon cumin** **½ teaspoon salt**	Place ground beef in 3-quart micro-proof casserole; break up with fork. Add onion, green pepper, and garlic. Cover. Cook on HI 5 to 6 minutes, stirring once during cooking time. Break up ground beef with fork; drain. Add remaining ingredients; mix lightly. Cover. Cook on HI 20 to 23 minutes, or until spaghetti is cooked, stirring every 10 minutes during cooking time. Let stand 5 minutes before serving.

Seafood Corn Chowder _____ 4 to 6 servings

Total Cooking Time: 20 to 24 minutes

4 slices bacon **½ cup chopped onion** **1 tablespoon minced** **green pepper** **1 can (16 ounces) cream-** **style corn** **1 can (10¾ ounces) cream** **of potato soup** **1 can (7½ ounces) minced** **clams, undrained** **1 can (4½ ounces) small** **shrimp, drained** **1½ cups milk** **¼ teaspoon white pepper** **1 tablespoon parsley** **flakes**	Place bacon in 3-quart microproof casserole. Cover with paper towels. Cook on HI 4 to 5 minutes, or until crisp. Remove bacon with slotted spoon; set aside. Drain all but 1 tablespoon bacon drippings from casserole. Add onion and green pepper. Cover. Cook on HI 4 minutes, or until onion is transparent. Stir in corn, potato soup, clams, shrimp, milk, pepper, and parsley. Cover. Cook on 70 for 12 to 15 minutes, or until hot, stirring twice during cooking time. Sprinkle bacon pieces on individual servings. Serve hot.

Lentil Soup ——————————— 6 servings

Total Cooking Time: 60 minutes

1 cup dried lentils, rinsed
6 cups hot water, divided
**½ pound smoked sausage,
cut into ½-inch slices**
¼ cup diced celery
**1 medium carrot, thinly
sliced**
¼ teaspoon salt
**¼ teaspoon freshly ground
pepper**
1 clove garlic, minced
1 bay leaf

Combine lentils and 4 cups of the water in 3-quart microproof casserole; let stand at room temperature overnight. Add sausage, celery, carrot, salt, pepper, garlic, and bay leaf; stir. Cover. Cook on HI 1 hour, stirring after 25 minutes. Add remaining 2 cups hot water. Discard bay leaf and serve.

Meatball Soup ——————————— 4 to 6 servings

Total Cooking Time: 16 to 18 minutes

**1 can (28 ounces) whole
tomatoes, broken up**
½ cup water
1 small onion, diced
1 clove garlic, minced
**1 tablespoon chopped
green pepper**
1 teaspoon chili powder
½ teaspoon salt
¼ teaspoon marjoram
**¼ teaspoon freshly ground
pepper**
½ pound lean ground beef
¼ pound ground pork
½ cup cornmeal
1 egg

Combine tomatoes, water, onion, garlic, chilies, chili powder, salt, marjoram, and pepper in 2-quart microproof bowl. Cover with plastic wrap. Cook on HI 5 minutes. In separate bowl, combine remaining ingredients; blend well. Shape into ½-inch meatballs. Drop meatballs into soup. Cook on HI 11 to 13 minutes, or until meatballs are no longer red, stirring after 5 minutes. Let stand 5 minutes before serving.

Turkey Soup _____ 4 to 6 servings

Total Cooking Time: 55 to 63 minutes

**1 to 1½ pounds turkey
   wings**
4 cups water
1 cup chopped onions
½ cup thinly sliced carrots
½ cup thinly sliced celery
1 bay leaf
1 teaspoon salt
**⅛ teaspoon freshly ground
   pepper**

Combine all ingredients in 3-quart microproof bowl. Cover. Cook on HI 22 to 25 minutes, or until mixture is boiling. Rearrange turkey. Cook on 50 for 30 to 35 minutes, or until turkey is tender, adding more water if necessary, to keep turkey covered. Remove turkey from broth with slotted spoon. Let stand until cool enough to handle; remove and discard bone and skin. Cut meat into bite-size pieces; return to broth. Discard bay leaf. Cook on HI 3 minutes, or until heated through. Serve immediately.

Tuna-Vegetable Soup _____ 3 to 4 servings

Total Cooking Time: 33 to 35 minutes

2 cups water
**1 medium potato, peeled
   and sliced**
¼ cup chopped onion
¼ cup diced carrot
¼ cup sliced celery
1 teaspoon chopped chives
**1 teaspoon Worcestershire
   sauce**
½ teaspoon salt
**3 cubes chicken bouillon
   Dash freshly ground
   pepper**
**¾ cup fresh or frozen corn,
   (thaw, if frozen)**
**1 can (7 ounces) tuna,
   drained and flaked**
**1 cup light cream or
   half-and-half**

Combine water, potato, onion, carrot, celery, chives, Worcestershire, salt, bouillon, and pepper in 3-quart microproof casserole. Cover. Cook on HI 15 minutes, or until all vegetables are tender. Add corn. Cover. Cook on HI 15 minutes, or until corn is tender. Stir in tuna and cream. Cover. Cook on 70 for 3 to 5 minutes, or until heated through. Stir; let stand 5 minutes before serving.

To reduce calories, substitute 1 cup evaporated low-fat milk for 1 cup light cream.

Hearty Cheese and Frank Soup _____ 6 servings

Total Cooking Time: 22 to 23 minutes

¼ **cup butter or margarine**
½ **cup sliced celery**
1 **carrot, diced**
¼ **cup chopped onion**
2 **tablespoons all-purpose flour**
2 **cans (14½ ounces each) condensed chicken broth**
½ **pound frankfurters, sliced**
2 **cups (8 ounces) shredded Cheddar cheese**
1½ **cups milk or half-and-half**

Combine butter, celery, carrot, and onion in 3-quart microproof casserole. Cover. Cook on HI 7 to 8 minutes, or until vegetables are tender, stirring once during cooking time. Blend in flour until smooth. Stir in chicken broth and frankfurters. Cover. Cook on HI 10 minutes, or until heated through, stirring once during cooking time. Add cheese; stir until melted. Add milk. Cover. Cook on 50 for 5 minutes, or until heated through.

Quick Minestrone _____ 8 servings

Total Cooking Time: 32 to 34 minutes

1½ **cups cubed cooked beef or ham**
1 **can (16 ounces) tomatoes, broken up, undrained**
1 **can (15 ounces) kidney beans, undrained**
1 **can (10¾ ounces) condensed tomato soup**
1 **cup water**
½ **cup shredded cabbage**
½ **cup uncooked vermicelli, broken in 1-inch pieces**
1 **clove garlic, minced**
1 **tablespoon Worcestershire sauce**
½ **teaspoon salt**
½ **teaspoon basil**
¼ **teaspoon freshly ground pepper**
Grated Parmesan cheese

Combine all ingredients, except Parmesan cheese, in 3-quart microproof casserole. Cover. Cook on HI 32 to 34 minutes, or until vermicelli is cooked, stirring twice during cooking time. Let stand 10 minutes. Serve in bowls sprinkled with Parmesan cheese.

Manhattan Seafood Chowder ———— 5 to 6 servings

Total Cooking Time: 13 to 16 minutes

**1 package (16 ounces)
    frozen cod, flounder
    or haddock fillets**
2 tablespoons vegetable oil
**1 medium green pepper,
    seeded and cut in
    thin strips**
1 small onion, sliced
1 clove garlic, minced
**1 can (16 ounces)
    tomatoes**
**1 bottle (8 ounces)
    clam juice**
¼ teaspoon basil
¼ teaspoon salt
⅛ teaspoon white pepper
**1 can (10 ounces) minced
    clams, undrained**

Partially thaw frozen fish per instructions (page 131). Cut into chunks and set aside. Combine oil, green pepper, onion, and garlic in 3-quart microproof bowl. Cook on HI 3 minutes, stirring once. Add fish, tomatoes, clam juice, basil, salt, and pepper. Cook on HI 8 to 10 minutes. Add clams and liquid; stir. Cook on HI 2 to 3 minutes, or until heated through and fish flakes easily.

Cream of Mushroom Soup ———— 4 to 6 servings

Total Cooking Time: 8 minutes

**2 tablespoons butter or
    margarine**
1 cup sliced mushrooms
1 small onion, diced
**1 cup chicken bouillon or
    broth**
**2 tablespoons all-purpose
    flour**
¼ teaspoon white pepper
¼ teaspoon nutmeg
1 cup milk

Combine butter, mushrooms, and onion in 2-quart microproof bowl. Cover with plastic wrap. Cook on HI 3 minutes, or until onion is transparent. Add remaining ingredients, except milk. Cook on HI 2 minutes. Stir in milk. Cover. Cook on 70 for 3 minutes. Let stand 2 minutes before serving.

Manhattan Seafood Chowder ➔

Beef Vegetable Soup ———————— 8 servings
Total Cooking Time: 31 to 35 minutes

1 pound lean ground beef
4 cups water
1 can (16 ounces)
   tomatoes, broken up,
   liquid reserved
1 package (10 ounces)
   frozen mixed
   vegetables, thawed
1 cup uncooked noodles
1 envelope onion soup mix
1 bay leaf
1 teaspoon salt
⅛ teaspoon freshly ground pepper

Place ground beef in 3-quart micro-proof casserole; break up with fork. Cook on HI 4 to 5 minutes, or until beef is no longer red, stirring once during cooking. Break up ground beef with fork; drain. Stir in remaining ingredients. Cover. Cook on HI 27 to 30 minutes, or until mixture boils and noodles are cooked, stirring every 10 minutes. Let stand, covered, 10 minutes. Discard bay leaf before serving.

Onion-Beef Soup ———————— 6 servings
Total Cooking Time: 20 to 23 minutes

3 medium onions, thinly
   sliced
¼ cup butter or margarine
4 cups beef broth
1 teaspoon Worcestershire
   sauce
1 teaspoon salt
1 teaspoon soy sauce
½ teaspoon paprika
   Grated Parmesan cheese

Combine onions and butter in 3-quart microproof casserole. Cover. Cook on HI 10 to 12 minutes, or until onions are transparent, stirring once during cooking time. Stir in remaining ingredients, except cheese. Cook on HI 10 to 11 minutes, or until hot. Serve in bowls with cheese sprinkled on top.

Lemon Chicken Rice Soup ———————— 4 servings
Total Cooking Time: 20 to 21 minutes

4 cups chicken broth
¼ cup quick-cooking rice
3 eggs
3 tablespoons lemon juice
1 cup minced cooked
   chicken

Pour broth into 2-quart glass measure. Cook on HI 17 minutes. Add rice. Cover and let stand 5 minutes. Beat eggs until foamy. Beat in lemon juice. Gradually add 1 cup hot broth to egg mixture, beating constantly. Stir egg mixture into remaining hot broth. Cook on 60 for 2 to 3 minutes, or until soup is thickened, stirring every 2 minutes. Stir in chicken. Cook on 60 for 1 minute. Serve in bowls garnished with a lemon slice, if desired.

Hot Dog Cheese Wrap _____ 2 servings

Total Cooking Time: 3 to 3½ minutes

2 slices bacon
2 hot dog buns
1 tablespoon mustard
1 slice Cheddar cheese
2 hot dogs

Place bacon between 2 sheets of paper towels. Cook on HI 2 minutes, or until partially cooked. Split buns; spread with mustard; set aside. Cut cheese into eight ¼-inch strips; divide cheese into 2 stacks. Cut each hot dog lengthwise in half, almost through. Lay cheese strips in slit. Wrap bacon strip around each hot dog. Place hot dogs in buns. Wrap each with paper towel. Cook on 80 for 1 to 1½ minutes. Let stand 1 minute before serving.

For the unadorned-dog lover, you can cook a plain hot dog just as quickly and easily. Score hot dog, place on micro-proof plate, and cook on 80 for 50 seconds. Place in bun and cook on 80 for 10 seconds. For 2 hot dogs, cook 1 to 1½ minutes before adding buns; 3 hot dogs, 1½ to 2 minutes; 4 hot dogs, 2 to 2¼ minutes.

Beef Tacos and Fixin's _____ 8 servings

Total Cooking Time: 8 minutes

1 pound lean ground beef
½ cup chopped onion
1 clove garlic, minced
½ cup tomato juice
1 package (1¼ ounces) taco seasoning mix
8 taco shells
2 cups shredded lettuce
2 medium tomatoes, chopped
1½ cups shredded Cheddar cheese
1 medium onion, finely chopped
1 avocado, diced

Place beef in 2-quart microproof casserole; break up with fork. Add onion and garlic. Cover and cook on HI 4 minutes, or until beef is no longer red, stirring several times during cooking time; drain. Stir in juice and taco seasoning. Cook on HI 3 minutes, or until heated through. Arrange taco shells on microproof plate. Cook on HI 1 minute. Divide beef mixture, lettuce, tomatoes, cheese, onion, and avocado among shells. Serve with a favorite hot sauce, if desired.

Cream of Broccoli Soup ———————— 4 to 6 servings

Total Cooking Time: 13 to 14 minutes

1 **can (14½ ounces)
    chicken broth**
1 **cup milk**
2 **tablespoons butter or
    margarine**
2 **tablespoons cornstarch**
½ **teaspoon salt**
½ **teaspoon parsley flakes**
¼ **teaspoon white pepper**
¼ **teaspoon nutmeg**
1½ **cups finely chopped
    broccoli**

Combine all ingredients, except broccoli, in 2-quart microproof bowl. Stir until cornstarch is dissolved. Add broccoli. Cover with plastic wrap. Cook on 70 for 13 to 14 minutes, or until broccoli is fork tender. Stir once during cooking time. Let stand 3 minutes before serving. Garnish with small raw broccoli floret.

Frank Reuben ————————————————— 4 servings

Total Cooking Time: 4 to 5 minutes

   Butter or margarine
4 **slices dark rye bread,
    toasted**
6 **frankfurters, sliced
    lengthwise in half**
1 **can (8 ounces) sauerkraut,
    drained**
4 **tablespoons Thousand
    Island dressing**
4 **slices Swiss cheese**

Lightly butter toast. Arrange 3 frankfurter halves on each toast slice. Divide sauerkraut among sandwiches. Spoon 1 tablespoon dressing on each. Top with 1 slice Swiss cheese. Wrap each sandwich in paper towels. Place 2 sandwiches on microproof plate. Cook on HI 2 to 2½ minutes, or until cheese is melted and sandwich is hot. Repeat with remaining sandwiches. Top with additional dressing, if desired.

Cream of Broccoli Soup, Frank Reuben   ➡

Super Sandwich _____ 1 serving

Total Cooking Time: 3 to 4 minutes

**1 slice (1-inch thick)
     Italian bread or 1
     large hard roll, split**
**1 tablespoon butter or
     margarine**
1 slice bologna
1 slice summer sausage
⅓ cup sauerkraut, drained
**1 slice mozzarella cheese
     Paprika**

Spread bread with butter. Cut bologna and sausage in half. Alternate meat slices on bread. Top with sauerkraut. Top with cheese. Place sandwich on paper towel-lined microproof plate. Cook on 30 for 3 to 4 minutes, or until cheese is melted and sandwich is heated through. Sprinkle with paprika. Let stand 1 minute before serving.

To heat 4 sandwiches, arrange in circle on plate. Cook on 30 for 10 to 12 minutes.

Tomato, Cheese, and
Bacon Sandwich _____ 2 servings

Total Cooking Time: 3½ to 4 minutes

2 slices bacon
2 slices rye bread, toasted
1½ tablespoons mayonnaise
¼ teaspoon dillweed
1 medium tomato, sliced
**2 slices Swiss or Cheddar
     cheese**

Place bacon between paper towels on microproof plate. Cook on HI 2 minutes, or until crisp. Spread toast with mayonnaise; sprinkle with dillweed. Place toast on paper towel-lined microproof plate. Top with slice each of tomato and cheese. Break bacon slices in half; place 2 halves on each sandwich. Cook on 60 for 1½ to 2 minutes, or until cheese is melted. Serve hot.

Cheeseburgers ———————————— 4 servings

Total Cooking Time: 5 to 6½ minutes

1 pound lean ground beef
Garlic salt
Freshly ground pepper
4 hamburger buns, split
and toasted
4 slices process American
cheese

Season ground beef with garlic salt and pepper. Shape into 4 patties. Arrange in 10-inch round microproof baking dish. Cover with waxed paper. Cook on HI 2 minutes. Turn patties over; season. Cover. Cook on HI 2 to 3 minutes, until desired degree of doneness.

Place patties on bottoms of hamburger buns. Top each with slice of cheese. Place cheeseburgers in a circle on 10-inch paper towel-lined microproof plate. Cook on 80 for 1 to 1½ minutes, or until cheese is melted. Cover with tops of buns. Let stand 1 minute before serving.

Bacon and Tomato Rabbit ——————— 4 servings

Total Cooking Time: 11 to 12½ minutes

4 slices bacon
1 can (10¾ ounces) cream
of tomato soup
1 teaspoon Worcestershire
sauce
1 teaspoon prepared
mustard
⅛ teaspoon cayenne
½ pound American process
cheese, cut up
1 egg, slightly beaten
4 slices tomato
2 English muffins, split
and toasted, or
4 rusks, buttered

Place bacon between paper towels on microproof plate. Cook on HI 4 to 4½ minutes, or until crisp; set aside.

Combine soup, Worcestershire, mustard, cayenne, and cheese in 4-cup glass measure. Cook on 50 for 6 to 7 minutes, or until cheese is melted, stirring twice during cooking time. Stir small amount of cheese mixture into egg, then return egg mixture to cheese, stirring briskly; set aside.

Arrange tomato slices on microproof plate. Cook on HI 1 minute, or until warm. Place English muffin halves on individual serving plates. Top each with tomato slice. Break bacon in half; place on tomato slices. Spoon cheese sauce over all. Serve immediately.

Tuna, Tomato, and Cheese ———————— 6 servings

Total Cooking Time: 2 to 3 minutes

**3 English muffins, split
and toasted
3 tablespoons butter or
margarine
1 large tomato, cut into
6 slices
1 can (6½ ounces) tuna,
drained and flaked
2 tablespoons mayonnaise
3 slices Cheddar or Swiss
cheese**

Spread muffins with butter. Arrange in circle on large paper towel-lined microproof plate. Place tomato slice on each muffin. Mix tuna and mayonnaise until blended. Divide and spoon tuna over tomato slices. Cut cheese diagonally in half to form triangles. Place 1 triangle of cheese on each muffin. Cook on 80 for 2 to 3 minutes, or until cheese is melted and muffin topping is warm. Let stand 2 minutes before serving.

A single split muffin can be prepared and cooked on 80 for 30 to 45 seconds. Toasted bread can be substituted for English muffins.

Chicken Croissants ———————————— 2 servings

Total Cooking Time: 1¾ to 2½ minutes

**¾ cup chopped cooked
chicken (one-half
breast)
1 hard-cooked egg,
chopped
¼ cup finely chopped
celery
3 tablespoons mayonnaise
2 tablespoons thinly
sliced green onion
1 tablespoon chopped
parsley
¼ teaspoon dillweed
Salt and freshly ground
pepper
2 croissants
2 slices (1 ounce each)
Monterey Jack cheese**

Combine chicken, egg, celery, mayonnaise, green onion, parsley, dillweed, salt, and pepper in mixing bowl; blend well. Set aside. Cut croissants in half lengthwise. Place bottom halves on microproof plate. Top each with half of the chicken mixture. Place 1 slice cheese on each croissant. Cook on 80 for 1½ to 2 minutes. Cover with top halves of croissants. Cook on 80 for 15 to 30 seconds.

Here are some other suggestions for croissant fillings: tuna salad, ham salad, pastrami and sauerkraut (squeeze all moisture from sauerkraut), sliced hot dogs and chili, and spinach with mushrooms and cheese. Now it's your turn!

A LA CARTE

Asparagus and broccoli, arranged for cooking. Split the broccoli stalks (right). Use 30 and cook 1 minute to warm cheese. Cook on HI 1 minute to melt cheese (above).

Here's where you'll find all the special side dishes that help to make a banquet out of any entrée. You'll also discover the microwave method for "special order" and traditional egg or cheese dishes. And you're sure to conclude that there's nothing quite like scrambled eggs or cheese fondue made in the microwave oven.

Vegetables, too, will cook beautifully in your oven. Just think — little water, and sometimes none at all, is used when cooking vegetables in the microwave. They don't lose any vitamins and maintain that just-picked flavor and color.

Potatoes? You bet. There's no more dramatic example of microwave cooking speed than a baked potato that took all of 4 to 6 minutes to cook!

But, let's face it, nothing is absolutely perfect. Pasta and rice cook fine in the microwave, but no time is saved. That's because they must be reconstituted, and there's no way to shorten the conventional timing. They do reheat incredibly well, however.

Converting Your Recipes

As you convert, consider that vegetables are at their best when served crisp-tender, as in wok cooking. For a softer texture, however, simply add a bit more water and increase cooking time until they reach the texture you prefer. All vegetables are cooked on HI. To convert that family favorite, simply find a similar recipe here or look for timing hints in the Guides.

☐ You can use a microwave thermometer when cooking most vegetable dishes. 150°F is the usually preferred temperature for doneness.

☐ Pasta, rice, and cereals are best when added to other ingredients, as in vegetable, meat, or cheese casseroles. While the oven can cook them separately, there's no advantage. It is wise to reheat them in the oven, however. You add no water, and they are like fresh cooked. Cook on HI 3 to 4 minutes for 1 cup (cooked), 5 to 6 minutes for 2 cups, etc. Cover tightly.

☐ Grits or other hot cereals are interesting side dishes for brunch, cooked in individual bowls. Cook on HI 6 to 7 minutes for ⅔ cup grits (uncooked); 1 to 2 minutes for ⅓ cup quick oatmeal. Follow package directions for liquid.

☐ To reheat mashed potatoes, cook on 80 for 2 to 3 minutes.

☐ To cook mashed potatoes, cube potatoes. Add a small amount of water. Cook, tightly covered, until soft. Season and mash.

☐ Eggs are undercooked slightly and allowed to complete cooking during standing time. Eggs are cooked covered to trap steam and assure even cooking.

Arrange asparagus with the tender tips overlapped in the center of the dish. Carrots cook a bit more quickly and are more interesting when cut diagonally. For best results, when cutting vegetables for cooking, make sizes as uniform as possible.

COOKING GUIDE — SCRAMBLED EGGS
Use Power Control 60

Number of Eggs	Liquid (Milk or Cream)	Butter	Minutes to Cook
1	1 tablespoon	1 teaspoon	1 to 1½
2	2 tablespoons	2 teaspoons	2 to 2½
4	3 tablespoons	3 teaspoons	4½ to 5½
6	4 tablespoons	4 teaspoons	7 to 8

• Break eggs into a microproof bowl or glass measure. Add milk or cream. Beat with a fork. Add butter. Cover with waxed paper. Stir at least once during cooking from the outside to the center. Let stand 1 minute before serving.

COOKING GUIDE — POACHED EGGS
Use HI for water, 50 after adding egg

Number of Eggs	Water	Container	Minutes to Boil Water	Minutes to Cook
1	¼ cup	6-ounce microproof custard cup	1½ to 2	1
2	¼ cup	6-ounce microproof custard cups	2	1½ to 2
3	¼ cup	6-ounce microproof custard cups	2 to 2½	2 to 2½
4	1 cup	1-quart microproof dish	2½ to 3	2½ to 3

• Bring water to a boil with a pinch of salt and up to ¼ teaspoon vinegar. Break egg carefully into hot water. Pierce egg lightly with toothpick. Cover with waxed paper. Let stand, covered, 1 minute before serving.

COOKING GUIDE — RICE

Food	Amount Uncooked	Water	Power Control Setting	Time (minutes)	Standing Time (minutes)	Special Notes
Short-grain	1 cup	2 cups	HI	12 - 15	5	3-quart casserole.
Long-grain	1 cup	2 cups	HI	14 - 17	5	3-quart casserole.
Wild rice	1 cup	3 cups	50	40 - 45	5	3-quart casserole.
Brown rice	1 cup	3 cups	50	45 - 50	5	3-quart casserole.
Quick-cooking	1 cup	1 cup	HI	3 - 4	5	1-quart casserole.

• Add salt and butter or margarine according to package directions. Cover tightly. Let stand, covered, 5 minutes before serving.

Vegetable Cooking Tips

1. Use a wide, shallow dish so vegetables can be spread out.
2. Cover all vegetables tightly.
3. Slit pouches of frozen vegetables to provide steam vents, and cook in microproof dish.
4. Most frozen vegetables can be cooked in their cartons without water. Remove waxed paper wrapping before placing carton in oven. Frozen vegetables in foil-lined cartons and frozen-in-sauce vegetables must be removed from cartons and placed in microproof baking dish or casserole. Add liquid, as package directs, before cooking.
5. After cooking, allow all vegetables to stand, covered, 2 to 3 minutes.

COOKING GUIDE — VEGETABLES
Use HI

Food	Amount	Vegetable Preparation	Time (minutes)	Water	Special Notes
Artichokes 3½" in diameter	Fresh: 1 2 4 Frozen: 10 oz.	Wash thoroughly. Cut tops off each leaf. Slit pouch.	7 - 8 11 - 12 5 - 6	¼ cup ½ cup 1 cup	When done, a leaf peeled from whole comes off easily.
Asparagus; spears and cut pieces	Fresh: 1 lb. Frozen: 10 oz.	Wash thoroughly. Snap off tough base and discard.	2 - 3 7 - 8	¼ cup None	Stir or rearrange once during cooking time.
Beans: green, wax, French-cut	Fresh: 1 lb. Frozen: 6 oz.	Remove ends. Wash well. Leave whole or break in pieces.	12 - 14 7 - 8	¼ cup None	Stir once or rearrange as necessary.
Beets	4 medium	Scrub beets. Leave 1" of top on beet.	16 - 18	¼ cup	After cooking, peel. Cut or leave whole.
Broccoli	Fresh, whole 1 - 1½ lbs. Frozen, whole Fresh, chopped 1 - 1½ lbs. Frozen, chopped 10 oz.	Remove outer leaves. Slit stalks.	9 - 10 8 - 10 12 - 14 8 - 9	¼ cup ¼ cup ¼ cup None	Stir or rearrange during cooking time.
Brussels sprouts	Fresh: 1 lb. Frozen: 10 oz.	Remove outside leaves if wilted. Cut off stems. Wash.	8 - 9 6 - 7	¼ cup None	Stir or rearrange once during cooking time.
Cabbage	½ medium head, shredded 1 medium head, wedges	Remove outside wilted leaves.	5 - 6 13 - 15	¼ cup ¼ cup	Rearrange wedges after 7 minutes.

Food	Amount	Vegetable Preparation	Time (minutes)	Water	Special Notes
Carrots	4: sliced or diced	Peel and cut off tops.	7 - 9	1 Tb.	Stir once during cooking time.
	6: sliced or diced	Fresh young carrots cook best.	9 - 10	2 Tbs.	
	8: tiny, whole		8 - 10	2 Tbs.	
	Frozen: 10 oz.		8 - 9	None	
Cauliflower	1 medium, in flowerets	Cut tough stem. Wash, remove outside leaves. Remove core.	7 - 8	¼ cup	Stir after 5 minutes.
	1 medium, whole		8 - 9	½ cup	Turn over once.
	Frozen: 10 oz.		8 - 9	¼ cup	Stir after 5 minutes.
Celery	2½ cups, 1" slices	Clean stalks thoroughly.	8 - 9	¼ cup	
Corn: kernel	Frozen: 10 oz.		5 - 6	⅓ cup	Stir halfway through cooking time.
On the cob	1 ear	Husk. Cook no more than 4 at a time.	3 - 4	None	Place in microproof dish. Add ¼ cup water. Cover with plastic wrap. After cooking, let stand, covered, 2 minutes.
	2 ears		6 - 7	None	
	3 ears		9 - 10	None	
	4 ears		11 - 12	None	
	Frozen, 2 ears	Flat dish, covered.	5½ - 6	None	Rearrange halfway through cooking time.
	4 ears		10 - 11	None	
Eggplant	1 medium, sliced	Wash and peel. Cut in slices or cubes.	5 - 6	2 Tb.	
	1 medium, whole	Pierce skin.	6 - 7		Place on microwave rack.
Greens: collard, kale, etc.	Fresh: 1 lb.	Wash. Remove wilted leaves or tough stem.	6 - 7	None	
	Frozen: 10 oz.		7 - 8	None	
Mushrooms	Fresh: ½ lb., sliced	Add butter.	2 - 4	2 Tbs.	Stir halfway through cooking time.
Okra	Fresh: ½ lb.	Wash thoroughly. Leave whole or cut in thick slices.	3 - 5	¼ cup	
	Frozen: 10 oz.		7 - 8	None	
Onions	1 lb., tiny whole	Peel. Add 1 Tb. butter.	6 - 7	¼ cup	Stir once during cooking time.
	1 lb., medium to large	Peel and quarter. Add 1 Tb. butter.	7 - 9	¼ cup	
Parsnips	4 medium, quartered	Peel and cut.	8 - 9	¼ cup	Stir once during cooking time.
Peas: green	Fresh: 1 lb.	Shell peas. Rinse well.	7 - 8	¼ cup	Stir once during cooking time.
	Fresh: 2 lbs.		8 - 9	½ cup	
	Frozen: 6 oz.		5 - 6	None	
Peas and onion	Frozen: 10 oz.		6 - 8	2 Tbs.	
Pea pods	Frozen: 6 oz.		3 - 4	2 Tbs.	
Potatoes, Sweet 5 - 6 oz. ea.	1	Scrub well. Pierce with fork. Place on rack or paper towel in circle, 1" apart.	4 - 4½	None	
	2		6 - 7	None	
	4		8 - 10	None	
	6		10 - 11	None	

Food	Amount	Vegetable Preparation	Time (minutes)	Water	Special Notes
Potatoes, white baking 6 - 8 oz. ea.	1 2 3 4 5	Wash and scrub well. Pierce with fork. Place on rack or paper towel in circle, 1" apart.	4 - 6 6 - 8 8 - 12 12 - 16 16 - 20	None None None None None	
russet, boiling	3	Peel potatoes, cut in quarters.	12 - 16	½ cup	Stir once during cooking time.
Rutabaga	Fresh: 1 lb. Frozen: 10 oz.	Wash well. Remove tough stems or any wilted leaves.	6 - 7 7 - 8	None None	Stir once during cooking time.
Spinach	Fresh: 1 lb. Frozen: 10 oz.	Wash well. Remove tough stems. Drain.	6 - 7 7 - 8	None None	Stir once during cooking time.
Squash, acorn or butternut	1 - 1½ lbs. whole	Scrub. Pierce with fork.	10 - 12	None	Cut and remove seeds to serve.
Spaghetti squash	2 - 3 lbs.	Scrub, pierce with fork. Place on rack.	6 per lb.	None	Serve with butter, Parmesan cheese, or spaghetti sauce.
Turnips	4 cups cubed	Peel, wash.	9 - 11	¼ cup	Stir after 5 minutes.
Zucchini	3 cups sliced	Wash; do not peel. Add butter.	7 - 8	¼ cup	Stir after 4 minutes.

REHEATING GUIDE — CONVENIENCE VEGETABLES

Food	Amount	Power Control Setting	Time (minutes)	Special Notes
Au gratin vegetables, frozen	10 oz.	70	10 - 12	Microproof dish, covered.
Corn, scalloped frozen	12 oz.	70	7 - 8	1-quart microproof casserole, covered.
Potatoes stuffed, frozen	10 oz.	70	10 - 12	Shallow microproof dish. Cover with waxed paper.
Tator Tots, frozen				Follow package directions. Microproof baking dish. Rearrange once.
Creamed potato mix	4 - 5 oz.	70	20 - 24	
Au gratin, frozen	11½ oz.	70	10 - 12	1½-quart microproof casserole, covered.
Instant mashed	3½ oz. packet (4 servings)	HI	5 - 6	Use covered microproof casserole. **Follow package directions.** Reduce liquid by 1 tablespoon.
Vegetables, in pouch, frozen	10 - 12 oz.	HI	6 - 7	Slit pouch; place on microproof plate. Flex once during cooking time.
Stuffing mix	6 oz.	HI	8	1½-quart microproof casserole, covered. **Follow package directions.**

COOKING GUIDE — CANNED VEGETABLES

Size	Power Control Setting	Minutes Drained	Minutes Undrained	Special Notes
8 ounces	80	1½ - 2	2 - 2½	Regardless of quantity: use a 4-cup microproof casserole, covered. Stir once. Let stand, covered, 2 - 3 minutes before serving.
15 ounces	80	2½ - 3	3 - 4	
17 ounces	80	3½ - 4	4 - 5	

The Blanching Guide

The microwave oven can be a valuable and appreciated aid in preparing fresh vegetables for the freezer. (The oven is *not*, however, recommended for canning.) Follow these steps to blanch vegetables.

1. Measure amounts to be blanched; place by batches in microproof casserole.
2. Cover and cook on HI for time indicated on chart.
3. Stir vegetables halfway through cooking.
4. Let vegetables stand, covered, 1 minute after cooking.
5. Place vegetables in ice water at once to stop cooking. When vegetables feel cool, spread on towel to absorb excess moisture.
6. Package in freezer containers or pouches. Seal, label, date, and freeze.

BLANCHING GUIDE — VEGETABLES
Use HI

Food	Amount	Water	Approximate Time (minutes)	Casserole Size
Asparagus (cut in 1-inch pieces)	4 cups	¼ cup	4½	1½ quart
Beans, green or wax (cut in 1-inch pieces)	1 pound	½ cup	5	1½ quart
Broccoli (cut in 1-inch pieces)	1 pound	⅓ cup	6	1½ quart
Carrots (sliced)	1 pound	⅓ cup	6	1½ quart
Cauliflower (cut in flowerets)	1 head	⅓ cup	6	2 quart
Corn (cut from cob)	4 cups	none	4	1½ quart
Corn-on-the-cob (husked)	6 ears	none	5½	1½ quart
Onion (quartered)	4 medium	½ cup	3 - 4½	1 quart
Parsnips (cubed)	1 pound	¼ cup	2½ - 4	1½ quart
Peas (shelled)	4 cups	¼ cup	4½	1½ quart
Snow peas	4 cups	¼ cup	3½	1½ quart
Spinach (washed)	1 pound	none	4	2 quart
Turnips (cubed)	1 pound	¼ cup	3 - 4½	1½ quart
Zucchini (sliced or cubed)	1 pound	¼ cup	4	1½ quart

Acorn Squash with Peas _____ 4 servings

Total Cooking Time: 25 to 30 minutes

**2 acorn squash (1 to 1½
    pounds each)**
**1 package (10 ounces)
    frozen peas**
Salt
Freshly ground pepper
**1 jar (4 ounces) pimiento,
    drained**
**1 tablespoon butter or
    margarine**

Cook acorn squash according to Guide (page 70). Place package of peas on microproof plate. Cook on HI 4 to 5 minutes, or until thawed and warm. While peas are thawing, cut squash in half lengthwise; scoop out seeds. Place, cut-side up, on microproof plate. Sprinkle each half with salt and pepper. In small dish, mix peas, pimiento, and butter. Divide among squash halves. Cook on HI 1 minute. Serve hot.

Creamed Onions Williamsburg _____ 6 to 8 servings

Total Cooking Time: 18 to 22 minutes

**2 pounds fresh or thawed
    frozen small whole
    onions**
2 tablespoons water
**1 tablespoon butter or
    margarine**
**Basic White Sauce
    (page 77)**
**1 teaspoon chicken bouillon
    granules**
**1 teaspoon Worcestershire
    sauce**
¼ teaspoon marjoram
**⅛ teaspoon freshly ground
    pepper**
⅓ cup dairy sour cream
**2 tablespoons slivered
    almonds, toasted**

Combine onions, water, and butter in 2-quart microproof casserole. Cover. Cook on HI 10 to 11 minutes, or until onions are tender. Drain; set aside.

   Prepare Basic White Sauce. Add chicken bouillon, Worcestershire, marjoram, and pepper to White Sauce; stir. Cook on 70 for 1 minute. Stir sauce into onions. Cook on HI 3 to 5 minutes, or until hot. Blend ¼ cup of the sauce with sour cream. Stir sour cream into onion mixture. Sprinkle almonds on top. Serve hot.

Acorn Squash with Peas ➜

Carrot and Basil Bake _____ 6 servings
Total Cooking Time: 10 to 12 minutes

1 **pound carrots, peeled and shredded**
1 **small onion, minced**
2 **tablespoons butter or margarine**
2 **tablespoons water**
1 **teaspoon parsley flakes**
½ **teaspoon salt**
½ **teaspoon crushed sweet basil**

Combine all ingredients in 1¾-quart microproof casserole. Cover. Cook on HI 10 to 12 minutes, stirring twice during cooking time. Let stand 3 minutes before serving.

Zucchini Provencale _____ 6 servings
Total Cooking Time: 11 to 14 minutes

3 **medium zucchini, sliced (3 cups)**
2 **cups sliced fresh mushrooms**
⅔ **cup chopped onion**
1 **clove minced garlic**
2 **tablespoons butter or margarine**
2 **cans (6 ounces each) tomato paste**
⅔ **cup grated Parmesan cheese, divided**
1 **teaspoon salt**
⅛ **teaspoon freshly ground pepper**

Combine zucchini, mushrooms, onion, garlic, and butter in 2-quart microproof casserole. Cover. Cook on HI 8 to 10 minutes, or until vegetables are tender. Stir in tomato paste, ⅓ cup cheese, salt, and pepper. Sprinkle remaining cheese on top. Cook on 70 for 3 to 4 minutes, or until heated through and cheese is melted.

Braised Celery and Peas _____ 6 servings
Total Cooking Time: 12 to 15 minutes

2 **cups sliced celery, ¼-inch thick**
⅓ **cup chopped onion**
2 **tablespoons butter or margarine**
2 **tablespoons water**
½ **teaspoon salt**
¼ **teaspoon celery salt**
1 **package (10 ounces) frozen peas**
1 **tablespoon minced fresh parsley**

Combine celery, onion, butter, water, salt, and celery salt in 2-quart microproof casserole. Cover. Cook on HI 7 to 8 minutes, or until vegetables are tender, stirring once during cooking. Add peas. Cover. Cook on HI 5 to 7 minutes, stirring after 4 minutes. Sprinkle with parsley before serving.

Hot Spinach and Bacon ⸻ 4 servings

Total Cooking Time: 7½ to 10½ minutes

2 slices bacon
2 tablespoons chopped
onion
2 tablespoons vinegar
I tablespoon sugar
I package (10 ounces)
fresh spinach,
washed, drained,
stems removed

Place bacon in 3-quart microproof casserole. Cover with paper towels. Cook on HI 2 to 3 minutes, or until crisp. Remove bacon; cool and crumble. Drain all but I tablespoon drippings from casserole. Add onion. Cover. Cook on HI 1½ minutes, or until onion is transparent. Stir in vinegar and sugar. Add spinach; mix lightly. Cover. Cook on HI 4 to 6 minutes, or until spinach is tender, stirring once during cooking time; stir. Drain. Sprinkle with crumbled bacon. Serve hot.

Scalloped Corn ⸻ 6 to 8 servings

Total Cooking Time: 9 minutes

¼ cup butter or margarine
½ cup thinly sliced green
onions
2 cans (17 ounces each)
cream-style corn
½ teaspoon salt
¼ teaspoon ground thyme
I cup fresh bread cubes

Place butter and onions in 1½-quart microproof casserole. Cook on HI 3 minutes, or until onions are transparent. Add remaining ingredients, except bread cubes; blend well. Cook on HI 5 minutes; stir. Sprinkle bread cubes on top of corn. Cook on 80 for I minute. Let stand 2 minutes before serving.

Green Beans and Almonds ⸻ 3 to 4 servings

Total Cooking Time: 7½ to 8 minutes

I package (10 ounces)
frozen French-cut
green beans
½ cup slivered almonds
2 tablespoons butter or
margarine
½ teaspoon soy sauce

Set unopened package of beans on microproof plate. Cook on HI 5 minutes. Transfer to microproof serving dish; set aside. Combine almonds and butter in I-cup glass measure. Cook on HI 1½ to 2 minutes, or until almonds are slightly browned, stirring after I minute. Add soy sauce to almonds; stir into beans; toss lightly. Cook on HI I minute. Serve hot.

Asparagus with Mustard Sauce ———— 6 servings

Total Cooking Time: 5 to 6½ minutes

**1½ pounds fresh asparagus,
       cleaned and cut
       in pieces**
¼   cup water
⅓   cup mayonnaise
**1   tablespoon minced fresh
       parsley**
**1   teaspoon prepared
       mustard**
½   teaspoon onion salt
⅛   teaspoon white pepper

Combine asparagus and water in 2-quart microproof casserole. Cover. Cook on HI 4 to 5 minutes, or until tender, stirring once during cooking time; drain. Combine remaining ingredients, mixing lightly to coat asparagus. Cook on HI 1 to 1½ minutes, or until heated through.

Two packages (10 ounces each) frozen cut asparagus can be substituted for fresh asparagus; omit water. (See chart on page 68.)

Three Bean Bake ———————— 8 to 10 servings

Total Cooking Time: 17 to 20 minutes

2   slices bacon, diced
1   small onion, chopped
**1   can (31 ounces) pork and
       beans in tomato sauce**
**1   can (17 ounces) lima
       beans, drained**
**1   can (16 ounces) cut
       green beans, drained**
¼   cup catsup
**1   tablespoon prepared
       mustard**

Place bacon in 2-quart microproof casserole. Cover with paper towels. Cook on HI 2 to 3 minutes, or until crisp. Remove bacon; set aside, reserving drippings. Stir onion into drippings. Cover. Cook on HI 3 minutes, or until tender, stirring once during cooking. Add remaining ingredients; stir. Cover. Cook on HI 12 to 14 minutes. Top with reserved bacon and serve.

Corn-in-the-Husk ———————— 4 servings

Total Cooking Time: 11 to 12 minutes

4   ears corn in husks
Butter or margarine
Salt
Freshly ground pepper

Discard soiled outer portion of husk. Soak corn in cold water 10 minutes. Drain, but do not dry. Arrange corn in spoke fashion on microproof plate. Cook on HI 11 to 12 minutes, rearranging halfway through cooking time. Let stand 3 minutes. Peel and discard husks and silk. Serve with butter, salt, and pepper.

Broccoli and Sour Cream _____ 6 to 8 servings

Total Cooking Time: 14 to 15 minutes

- 1 **package (18 ounces)**
  frozen cut broccoli
- 2 **tablespoons chopped onion**
- 1 **tablespoon water**
- 1 **tablespoon butter or**
  margarine
- 1 **cup dairy sour cream**
- ½ **teaspoon celery salt**
- ¼ **teaspoon celery seed**
- ⅛ **teaspoon white pepper**

Combine broccoli, onion, water, and butter in 2-quart microproof casserole. Cook on HI 14 to 15 minutes, or until vegetables are tender, stirring once during cooking time. Drain, if necessary. Combine remaining ingredients; stir into broccoli. Cover and let stand 3 minutes before serving.

Creamed Cabbage _____ 6 servings

Total Cooking Time: 6 to 7 minutes

- 1 **teaspoon cornstarch**
- ½ **cup milk**
- 6 **cups shredded cabbage**
- 1 **package (3 ounces)**
  cream cheese, cut up
- 1 **tablespoon parsley flakes**
- 1 **tablespoon minced onion**
- 1 **teaspoon salt**
- ⅛ **teaspoon white pepper**

Dissolve cornstarch in milk. Combine all ingredients in 2-quart microproof casserole. Cover. Cook on HI 6 to 7 minutes, or until cabbage is tender, stirring once during cooking time. Stir and let stand 2 minutes before serving.

Basic White Sauce _____ 1 cup

Total Cooking Time: 4 to 5 minutes

- 2 **tablespoons butter**
- 2 **tablespoons all-purpose**
  flour
- 1 **cup milk**
  Dash white pepper
  Dash nutmeg

Place butter in 4-cup glass measure and cook on HI, 1 minute. Stir flour into butter until smooth. Whisk in milk, pepper, and nutmeg, blending well. Cook on HI, 2 minutes, stirring once. Whisk until smooth. Cook on HI, 1 to 2 minutes, or until thickened. Serve with cooked broccoli or cauliflower.

Potatoes Au Gratin _____ 4 to 5 servings
Total Cooking Time: 10 to 11 minutes

1 **package (16 ounces) frozen Southern-style hashed brown potatoes**
1 **can (10¾ ounces) condensed cream of potato soup**
½ **cup dairy sour cream**
¾ **cup shredded Cheddar cheese, divided**

Combine potatoes, soup, sour cream, and ½ cup cheese in 1¾-quart shallow microproof casserole; blend well. Cook on HI 10 to 11 minutes, or until potatoes are tender, stirring once during cooking time. Sprinkle with remaining ¼ cup cheese. Cover and let stand 3 minutes, or until cheese is melted.

Potato and Onion Casserole _____ 6 servings
Total Cooking Time: 9 to 11 minutes

2 **cups water**
2 **tablespoons butter or margarine**
½ **teaspoon salt**
¼ **teaspoon white pepper**
⅔ **cup milk**
2 **cups instant mashed potato flakes**
1 **egg, lightly beaten**
1 **package (3 ounces) cream cheese, quartered**
1 **can (3 ounces) French-fried onions, divided**

Combine water and butter in 2-quart microproof casserole. Cook on HI 5 to 6 minutes, or until boiling. Stir in salt, pepper, milk, and potato flakes; let stand 2 minutes. Add egg, cream cheese, and half of the onions; stir until cheese is melted. Cover. Cook on HI 4 to 5 minutes, or until heated through. Sprinkle with remaining onions. Serve hot.

Parslied Potatoes _____ 4 to 6 servings
Total Cooking Time: 12 to 14 minutes

4 **medium potatoes**
¼ **cup water**
3 **tablespoons butter or margarine**
3 **to 4 tablespoons minced fresh parsley**
Salt
Freshly ground pepper

Peel potatoes and quarter. Combine potatoes and water in 2-quart microproof casserole; cover. Cook on HI 12 to 14 minutes, or until tender, stirring once during cooking time; drain. Add butter, parsley, salt, and pepper. Stir until butter is melted. Serve immediately.

You may choose to use 16 whole new potatoes instead of quartering the larger variety.

Hashed Brown Potato Bake ⸻ 6 servings

Total Cooking Time: 15 to 17 minutes

1 **package (16 ounces) frozen Southern-style hashed browns**
1 **can (10¾ ounces) condensed cream of potato soup**
½ **cup dairy sour cream**
2 **green onions, sliced**
½ **teaspoon salt**
¼ **teaspoon freshly ground pepper**
1 **tablespoon minced fresh parsley**
  Paprika

Place frozen potatoes in 1½-quart microproof casserole. Cover. Cook on HI 5 minutes. Stir in soup, sour cream, onions, salt, pepper, and parsley. Cover. Cook on 70 for 10 to 12 minutes, stirring once during cooking time. Sprinkle with paprika. Let stand, covered, 5 minutes before serving.

Onion Pie in Rice Crust ⸻ 6 servings

Total Cooking Time: 19 to 21 minutes

1 **Rice Pie Crust (page 156)**
¾ **cup shredded Cheddar cheese**
¾ **cup shredded Swiss cheese**
¼ **cup thinly sliced green onion**
1 **tablespoon butter or margarine**
1 **can (5⅓ ounces) evaporated milk**
4 **eggs**
1 **teaspoon prepared mustard**
½ **teaspoon salt**
1 **can (3 ounces) French-fried onions**

Sprinkle cheeses in prepared pie crust. Combine onion and butter in 2-cup glass measure. Cook on HI 2 minutes, or until onion is transparent, stirring after 1 minute. Add milk. Cook on HI 2 minutes, or until milk is heated through.

Combine eggs, mustard, and salt in small bowl; mix lightly. Gradually pour hot milk mixture into egg mixture while beating. Pour carefully over cheese in pie crust. Crumble French-fried onions over top. Cook on 60 for 15 to 17 minutes, or until center is nearly set, rotating dish if pie is cooking unevenly. Cover with aluminum foil; let stand on breadboard or heatproof counter top 10 minutes before serving.

minutes before serving.

Brussels Sprouts with Walnut Butter
_____ 4 to 6 servings

Total Cooking Time: 14 to 20 minutes

1 pound fresh Brussels sprouts **3 tablespoons butter or margarine** **¼ cup chopped walnuts** **¼ cup water** **⅛ teaspoon freshly ground pepper**	Wash and trim Brussels sprouts. Soak in salted cold water 10 minutes; drain. Place butter in shallow microproof baking dish. Cover with waxed paper. Cook on HI 6 to 8 minutes, or until butter is browned. Stir in walnuts; set aside. Combine water and Brussels sprouts in 2-quart microproof casserole. Cover. Cook on HI 8 to 12 minutes, or until tender; drain. Place in serving dish. Pour walnut butter over top. Season with pepper. Serve hot.

Cauliflower Au Gratin
_____ 5 to 6 servings

Total Cooking Time: 9 to 11 minutes

1 medium head cauliflower **¼ cup water** **½ cup shredded mild Cheddar cheese** **¼ cup Italian seasoned bread crumbs**	Remove core from cauliflower; place upside down in 2-quart microproof casserole. Add water. Cover. Cook on HI 8 to 9 minutes, or until tender, turning over after 4 minutes. Drain, reserving liquid. Mix liquid with cheese and bread crumbs in small bowl. Spoon over cauliflower; pat gently. Cover. Cook on HI 1 to 2 minutes, or until cheese is melted. Let stand, covered, for 3 minutes before serving.

Candied Yams
_____ 4 to 6 servings

Total Cooking Time: 10½ to 12½ minutes

2 cans (23 ounces each) whole sweet potatoes, drained **1 large tart apple, cored and cut in wedges** **½ cup orange juice** **½ cup raisins** **¼ cup firmly packed brown sugar** **1 cup miniature marshmallows**	Arrange potatoes and apple wedges in 2-quart microproof casserole. Add remaining ingredients, except marshmallows. Cook on HI 8 to 10 minutes. Sprinkle with marshmallows. Cook on HI 2½ minutes, or until marshmallows are melted.

Brussels Sprouts with Walnut Butter, Cauliflower Au Gratin, Candied Yams ➜

Denver Scramble _____ 4 to 6 servings

Total Cooking Time: 6 to 7 minutes

4   eggs
¼   cup mayonnaise
¼   cup milk
½   cup minced cooked ham
**1   tablespoon instant
      minced onion**
**1   tablespoon chopped
      pimiento**
**1   tablespoon chopped
      green pepper**
⅛   teaspoon salt
**1   small tomato, seeded
      and chopped**
4   to 6 slices toast

Combine eggs, mayonnaise, and milk in 1- to 1½-quart microproof casserole; blend well. Stir in ham, onion, pimiento, green pepper, and salt. Cover. Cook on 60 for 5 to 6 minutes, or until just set, stirring every minute during cooking time. Stir in tomato. Cook on 60 for 1 minute. Let stand 2 minutes. Serve with toast.

_____

This recipe can be doubled and cooked in 2-quart microproof casserole. Double cooking time.

_____

Avocado Omelet _____ 2 servings

Total Cooking Time: 6 to 6½ minutes

**¾   cup finely diced ripe
      avocado**
1   tablespoon vegetable oil
**½   teaspoon Worcestershire
      sauce**
**½   teaspoon grated lemon
      rind**
**¼   teaspoon hot pepper
      seasoning**
4   eggs
4   tablespoons water
½   teaspoon salt
**⅛   teaspoon freshly ground
      pepper**
**1   tablespoon butter or
      margarine**
**1   tablespoon minced fresh
      parsley**

Combine avocado, oil, Worcestershire, lemon rind, and pepper seasoning in 2-cup glass measure. Let stand at room temperature about 1 hour. Combine eggs, water, salt, and pepper in mixing bowl; beat well; set aside. Place butter in 9-inch microproof pie plate. Cook on HI 1 minute, or until melted. Pour in egg mixture. Cover with waxed paper. Cook on 60 for 4 to 4½ minutes, or until almost set, stirring after 2 minutes and again after 4 minutes. Let stand, covered, 1 to 2 minutes.

To warm avocado mixture, cook on HI 1 minute. Spoon avocado mixture over half of omelet. Fold over other half of omelet. Remove omelet to serving platter. Spoon remaining avocado over top. Sprinkle with parsley. Cut in half. Serve hot.

Low-Cal Eggs Oriental ⸺ 2 to 3 servings

Total Cooking Time: 9½ to 11 minutes

1 **tablespoon butter or margarine**
½ **cup sliced mushrooms**
1 **cup chopped green onions**
4 **eggs**
4 **tablespoons water**
1 **can (8 ounces) sliced water chestnuts**
1 **cup alfalfa sprouts**
½ **teaspoon salt**
¼ **teaspoon freshly ground pepper**

Place butter in 8-inch microproof pie plate. Cook on HI 30 seconds, or until melted. Add mushrooms and onions. Cover with waxed paper. Cook on HI 2 minutes. Mix remaining ingredients in small bowl. Add to onions and mushrooms; stir lightly to mix. Cover. Cook on 60 for 7 to 8½ minutes, or until eggs are set, stirring every 2 minutes during cooking time. Let stand 1 to 2 minutes. Sprinkle with additional sprouts. Serve with soy sauce, if desired.

Eggs Sunny-Side-Up ⸺ 1 to 2 servings

Total Cooking Time: 4 to 4½ minutes

1 **tablespoon butter or margarine**
2 **eggs**
Dash salt
Freshly ground pepper

Place 9-inch browning dish in oven. Cook on HI 3 minutes to preheat dish. Add butter and allow to melt, tipping dish to coat entire surface. Break eggs into dish; pierce yolks. Sprinkle lightly with salt and pepper. Cover with glass lid. Cook on HI 1 to 1½ minutes, or until desired degree of doneness. Let stand 1 minute before serving.

Classic Omelet ⸺ 2 servings

Total Cooking Time: 6½ to 7 minutes

1 **tablespoon butter or margarine**
4 **eggs**
4 **tablespoons water**
½ **teaspoon salt**
⅛ **teaspoon freshly ground pepper**

Place butter in 9-inch microproof pie plate. Cook on HI 1 minute, or until melted. Beat remaining ingredients in bowl; pour into pie plate. Cover with waxed paper. Cook on 60 for 5½ to 6 minutes, stirring once during cooking time. Let stand, covered, 1 to 2 minutes. Fold in half to serve.

Palace Eggs ———————————————— 4 servings

Total Cooking Time: 8 to 11 minutes

5 tablespoons butter or margarine, divided
2 tablespoons all-purpose flour
⅛ teaspoon nutmeg
1¼ cups milk
1 package (2½ ounces) sliced smoked beef
4 eggs
4 tablespoons water
½ teaspoon salt
⅛ teaspoon freshly ground pepper
4 large rusks

Place 3 tablespoons of the butter in 4-cup glass measure. Cook on HI 1 minute, or until melted. Blend in flour and nutmeg. Stir in milk. Cook on HI 2 to 4 minutes, or until thickened, stirring every 1 minute. Snip beef into small pieces. Stir into sauce; set aside.

Break eggs into 4-cup glass measure; add water, salt, and pepper; beat to combine. Add 1 tablespoon of the butter. Cover with waxed paper. Cook on 60 for 4 to 5 minutes, stirring every minute.

Spread rusks with remaining 1 tablespoon butter; arrange on microproof serving plate. Divide and spoon eggs over rusks. Spoon beef sauce over eggs. Cook on 40 for 1 minute, or until hot. Serve immediately.

Cheddar Baked Eggs ———————————— 6 servings

Total Cooking Time: 9 to 10 minutes

2 tablespoons butter or margarine
6 eggs, lightly beaten
1 cup shredded Cheddar cheese
½ cup milk
½ teaspoon prepared mustard
½ teaspoon salt
Dash freshly ground pepper
Paprika

Place butter in 1½-quart microproof baking dish. Cook on HI 1 minute, or until melted. Combine eggs, cheese, milk, mustard, salt, and pepper in medium bowl; blend well. Pour into baking dish. Cover with waxed paper. Cook on 60 for 8 to 9 minutes, stirring after 3 minutes and again after 6 minutes. Sprinkle with paprika. Let stand 2 minutes before serving.

Crisp bacon slices make an especially nice addition to this hearty dish.

← *Palace Eggs, Cheddar Baked Eggs*

Welsh Rabbit on Toast ──────────── 4 to 6 servings
Total Cooking Time: 12 minutes

1   **pound (4 cups) shredded
    sharp Cheddar cheese**
4   **teaspoons butter or
    margarine**
¾   **teaspoon Worcestershire
    sauce**
½   **teaspoon paprika**
¼   **teaspoon salt**
¼   **teaspoon dry mustard**
¼   **teaspoon cayenne**
2   **large eggs, lightly beaten**
1   **cup flat beer or ale,
    at room temperature**
4   **to 6 slices French
    bread, toasted**

Combine cheese, butter, Worcestershire, paprika, salt, mustard, and cayenne in 2-quart microproof casserole. Cover. Cook on 50 for 6 minutes, stirring once during cooking time. Stir small amount of cheese mixture into eggs, then stir eggs back into cheese mixture. Mix in beer. Cover. Cook on 50 for 6 minutes, stirring once during cooking time. Stir thoroughly and briskly. Arrange toast in shallow bowls. Ladle cheese mixture over top and serve.

Noodles and Cheese ──────────── 4 to 6 servings
Total Cooking Time: 9 minutes

¼   **cup butter or margarine**
2   **cups shredded Swiss
    cheese**
1   **egg, lightly beaten**
½   **cup milk**
⅓   **cup slivered almonds**
1   **teaspoon parsley flakes**
¼   **teaspoon freshly ground
    pepper**
¼   **teaspoon nutmeg**
3   **cups cooked wide egg
    noodles**

Place butter in 1½-quart microproof casserole. Cook on HI 1 minute, or until melted. Combine melted butter and remaining ingredients, except noodles, in large mixing bowl. Add noodles; toss until separated and evenly coated. Place noodles in same casserole butter was melted in. Cover with plastic wrap. Cook on HI 8 minutes, stirring after 4 minutes. Let stand 2 minutes before serving.

Cheese Fondue ──────────── 4 to 6 servings
Total Cooking Time: 9 to 11 minutes

1   **pound (4 cups) shredded
    Swiss cheese**
2   **tablespoons cornstarch**
1½ **cups dry white wine**
1   **small clove garlic, minced
    Dash salt
    Freshly ground pepper
    French bread, cut in cubes
    Assorted vegetables**

Combine cheese and cornstarch in 2-quart microproof casserole. Stir in wine, garlic, salt, and pepper. Cook on 60 for 9 to 11 minutes, or until cheese is melted and smooth, stirring twice during cooking time. Pour into fondue pot and keep warm. If mixture becomes too thick, add more wine. Serve with bread cubes and assorted vegetables.

ONE-DISH DINNERS

Some casseroles need occasional stirring. Use hot pads when the dish is hot (left). Large items, such as chicken pieces, are rearranged using tongs (above).

By now, we think you should have a pretty good notion about the speed of microwave cooking. But let's not forget those time-saving, tasty casseroles, perhaps the first cooking shortcuts in conventional cooking. No doubt the first "casserole" was created in a cookpot over an open fire!

It probably won't surprise you to learn that the microwave oven is specially suited for cooking all kinds of casseroles. Convenience plus speed make those one-dish wonders better than ever.

Because no heat is applied to the casserole dish, food does not stick. And, of course, you can do ingredient preparation, such as sautéing onions or precooking meat, right in the same dish in the microwave oven. No stovetop steps at all!

We've assembled a balanced collection of some traditional casseroles and added a few unique ideas. We hope you will want to try all of them.

Converting Your Recipes

It's so easy to convert your own casserole recipes that you'll probably need to adjust only three items, if at all. They are: reducing the amount of liquid because little evaporation occurs in the microwave oven; changing from long-grain rice or dried beans or quick-cooking rice or precooked, canned beans; and, doing some steps first, such as cooking onion to be sure it is tender. For more help, read the casserole information on pages 26 and 27, along with these tips:

☐ Most ground beef casseroles call for extra-lean meat. If you are using regular ground beef, partially cook and then drain fat before adding other ingredients.

☐ Many casserole dishes have their own lids. However, often those lids, especially decorative ones, make large casseroles too tall for the oven. When necessary, cover with plastic wrap instead.

☐ With the microwave oven, casseroles can go right from the freezer to the oven for defrosting and cooking. For a 2-quart casserole, cook on 30 for 15 to 18 minutes. Let stand, covered, for 5 minutes. Stir. Cook on HI 10 to 13 minutes, stirring twice during cooking.

☐ A microwave thermometer can be used to determine precise casserole temperatures. 150°F is the recommended temperature.

Kielbasa and Cabbage ——————— 4 servings

Total Cooking Time: 16 to 18 minutes

1　**medium onion, sliced**
　　(about 1 cup)
1　**tablespoon butter or**
　　margarine
1　**pound kielbasa**
4　**cups shredded cabbage**
¾　**cup dairy sour cream**
2　**tablespoons Dijon mustard**
¼　**teaspoon salt**
⅛　**teaspoon freshly ground**
　　pepper

Combine onion and butter in 2-quart microproof casserole. Cook on 90 for 5 to 6 minutes, or until onion is transparent. Remove casing from kielbasa; slice ½-inch thick. Add cabbage and kielbasa to onion. Cover. Cook on HI 9 to 10 minutes, or until cabbage is cooked, stirring once during cooking time. Drain.

　　Combine sour cream, mustard, salt, and pepper in small bowl. Stir into cabbage mixture. Cover and cook on 70 for 2 minutes, or until heated through. Serve hot.

Ground Beef Gumbo _____ 4 to 5 servings

Total Cooking Time: 9 to 11 minutes

1 pound lean ground beef
¼ cup chopped onion
2 tablespoons chopped green pepper
1 can (10¾ ounces) chicken gumbo soup
¼ teaspoon salt
⅛ teaspoon freshly ground pepper
2 cups hot cooked rice

Combine beef, onion, and green pepper in 2-quart microproof casserole. Cook on HI 5 to 6 minutes, or until beef is no longer red, stirring once during cooking. Break up beef with fork; drain. Stir in remaining ingredients, except rice. Cover. Cook on HI 4 to 5 minutes, stirring once during cooking time. Serve over rice.

Spanish Rice Supper _____ 4 to 6 servings

Total Cooking Time: 19 to 21 minutes

1 pound lean ground beef
½ cup chopped onion
1 can (28 ounces) tomatoes, cut up, liquid reserved
1 cup quick-cooking rice
1 to 2 tablespoons chili powder
1 teaspoon salt
⅛ teaspoon freshly ground pepper

Place beef in 3-quart microproof casserole; break up with fork. Stir in onion. Cook on HI 7 minutes; drain. Add remaining ingredients; stir. Cover. Cook on HI 12 to 14 minutes, or until rice is tender, stirring once during cooking time. Stir and serve.

"Boiled" Dinner _____ 8 servings

Total Cooking Time: 60 to 65 minutes

1 corned beef brisket (2 to 3 pounds)
1 envelope onion soup mix
4 black peppercorns
1 clove garlic, halved
1 bay leaf
2 cups water
4 medium potatoes, peeled and quartered
4 medium carrots, peeled and cut in 1½-inch pieces

Cut a 1-inch strip from open end of cooking bag. Place brisket in bag; place in shallow microproof baking dish. Add soup, peppercorns, garlic, bay leaf, and water. (Add more water if necessary to cover completely.) Tie bag loosely with plastic strip. Cook on HI 20 minutes. Turn brisket; add potatoes and carrots. Cook on 50 for 15 minutes. Turn bag over. Cook on 50 for 25 to 30 minutes, or until brisket and vegetables are tender; add more water, if necessary. Discard bay leaf. Transfer brisket to platter; slice and surround with vegetables. Serve hot.

Sweet and Sour Shrimp Casserole

_____ 4 to 6 servings

Total Cooking Time: 14 to 16 minutes

3 tablespoons vegetable oil
1 medium onion, sliced
1 green pepper, seeded and cut into strips
1½ pounds fresh or frozen raw shrimp, peeled and deveined
1 can (16 ounces) pineapple chunks, drained; ½ cup syrup reserved
3 tablespoons cornstarch
⅓ cup firmly packed brown sugar
¼ cup soy sauce
¼ cup vinegar
¼ teaspoon ground ginger
¼ teaspoon freshly ground pepper
1 can (5 ounces) sliced water chestnuts, drained

Combine oil, onion, and green pepper in 3-quart microproof casserole. Cover. Cook on HI 4 minutes. Stir in shrimp. Cook on HI 1 minute. Set aside.

Pour reserved pineapple syrup into microproof bowl. Stir in cornstarch and all remaining ingredients, except water chestnuts and pineapple. Cook on HI 4 to 5 minutes, stirring twice during cooking time. Add shrimp, water chestnuts, and pineapple chunks. Cook on 80 for 5 to 6 minutes, or until heated through. Serve over hot cooked noodles or rice.

Beefburger Stroganoff

_____ 6 servings

Total Cooking Time: 13 to 15 minutes

1 pound lean ground beef
1 small onion, chopped
1 clove garlic, minced
1 can (10¾ ounces) condensed cream of chicken soup
1 can (8 ounces) mushroom stems and pieces, drained
2 tablespoons tomato paste
¼ teaspoon salt
⅛ teaspoon freshly ground pepper
1 cup dairy sour cream
2 tablespoons chopped fresh parsley
4 cups hot cooked rice or noodles

Place ground beef in 2-quart microproof casserole; break up with fork. Stir in onion and garlic. Cover and cook on HI 5 to 6 minutes, or until beef is no longer red and onion is transparent; drain. Stir in soup, mushrooms, tomato paste, salt, and pepper. Cover. Cook on HI 7 to 8 minutes, stirring once. Stir in sour cream. Cook on 60 for 1 minute; stir. Sprinkle with parsley. Serve over rice or noodles.

Sweet and Sour Shrimp Casserole ➔

Enchilada Chili Bake

6 to 8 servings

Total Cooking Time: 15 to 17 minutes

1   **pound lean ground beef**
1   **cup chopped onions**
1   **clove garlic, minced**
1   **can (10 ounces) hot enchilada sauce**
1   **can (8 ounces) tomato sauce**
1   **can (15 ounces) pinto beans**
2½ **cups crushed corn chips, divided**
1   **cup (4 ounces) shredded Cheddar cheese, divided**
1   **cup dairy sour cream**

Place beef in 3-quart microproof casserole; break up with spoon. Add onions and garlic. Cook on HI 5 to 6 minutes, or until beef is no longer red; drain. Stir again to break up beef.

Stir in enchilada sauce and tomato sauce. Cook on HI 3 minutes. Stir in beans, 1 cup of the corn chips, and ¾ cup of the cheese. Cover. Cook on HI 6 minutes; stir.

Spread sour cream evenly over top. Sprinkle remaining 1½ cups corn chips and ¼ cup cheese over sour cream. Cook on 70 for 1 to 2 minutes, or until sour cream is warm. Let stand 5 minutes before serving.

Quick Cassoulet

6 servings

Total Cooking Time: 11 to 14 minutes

1   **pound lean ground beef**
½   **pound smoked Polish sausage, casing removed, sliced in ½-inch pieces**
½   **cup chopped onion**
1   **clove garlic, minced**
1   **can (8 ounces) tomato sauce**
1   **bay leaf**
½   **teaspoon salt**
1   **can (15 ounces) Great Northern beans, drained**
½   **cup sliced celery**
⅓   **cup dry red wine**
1   **tablespoon all-purpose flour**
2   **tablespoons snipped parsley**

Place beef in 3-quart microproof casserole; break up with spoon. Add sausage, onion, and garlic. Cover. Cook on HI 5 to 6 minutes, or until beef is no longer red and onion is tender; drain; stir. Add tomato sauce, bay leaf, salt, beans, and celery.

Combine wine and flour in small bowl; blend well. Add to meat mixture; blend well. Cook on HI 6 to 8 minutes, or until heated through, stirring once during cooking time. Discard bay leaf. Sprinkle with parsley. Let stand 5 minutes before serving.

Supper Pie _____ 6 servings
Total Cooking Time: 15 to 17 minutes

1 **package (8 ounces) spaghetti, cooked**
1 **egg, lightly beaten**
⅓ **cup grated Parmesan cheese**
1 **tablespoon butter or margarine**
1 **tablespoon parsley flakes**
¾ **pound lean ground beef**
1 **onion, finely chopped**
1 **clove garlic, minced**
1 **can (8 ounces) whole tomatoes, drained and cut in pieces, liquid reserved**
1 **can (6 ounces) tomato paste**
½ **teaspoon oregano**
½ **teaspoon salt**
¼ **teaspoon freshly ground pepper**
1 **cup ricotta cheese**
½ **cup shredded Monterey Jack or mozzarella cheese**

Combine spaghetti, egg, Parmesan cheese, butter, and parsley in large bowl; stir until butter is melted. Turn into 10-inch microproof pie plate; press mixture evenly onto bottom and sides. Cook on HI 2 minutes, rotating after 1 minute; set aside.

Combine ground beef, onion, and garlic in 2-quart microproof bowl; break up beef with fork. Cook on HI 5 to 6 minutes, or until beef is no longer red; drain. Add tomatoes, tomato paste, oregano, salt, and pepper. Cook on HI 3 minutes.

Spread ricotta cheese over spaghetti; pour meat mixture over ricotta cheese. Cover with waxed paper. Cook on HI 5 to 6 minutes, or until heated through. Sprinkle with shredded cheese. Cover and let stand 3 minutes until cheese is melted. Serve hot.

Macaroni and Cheese _____ 4 to 6 servings
Total Cooking Time: 8 to 9 minutes

2 **cups elbow macaroni**
2 **tablespoons butter or margarine**
2 **tablespoons all-purpose flour**
2 **cups milk**
1 **teaspoon salt**
1 **tablespoon instant minced onion**
2 **cups shredded Cheddar cheese**

Cook macaroni according to package directions; drain. Place in 2-quart microproof casserole; set aside. Place butter in 2-quart glass measure. Cook on HI 1 minute, or until melted. Stir in flour until blended.

Pour milk into 2-cup glass measure. Cook on 70 for 2 minutes. Stir into flour-butter mixture. Cook on HI 5 to 6 minutes, or until thickened, stirring frequently. Add salt and onion. Add cheese; stir until melted. Pour over macaroni; blend well. Serve immediately.

Ham, Asparagus, and Noodle Casserole _____ 6 servings

Total Cooking Time: 9½ to 11½ minutes

2 cups cooked noodles
1 tablespoon parsley flakes
1 cup milk
2 tablespoons butter or margarine
2 tablespoons all-purpose flour
½ teaspoon salt
¼ teaspoon white pepper
1 package (3 ounces) cream cheese, cut up
3 teaspoons prepared mustard
6 slices boiled ham
1 can (14½ ounces) asparagus spears or 18 fresh asparagus spears, cooked and drained
Paprika

Combine noodles with parsley; mix lightly; set aside.

Pour milk into 2-cup glass measure. Cook on 70 for 2 minutes, or until heated through; set aside. Place butter in another 2-cup glass measure. Cook on HI 30 seconds. Stir in flour; blend well. Cook on HI 1 minute. Briskly stir in warm milk, salt, and pepper. Cook on HI 2 to 3 minutes, or until boiling and thickened, stirring once during cooking. Stir in cream cheese until melted.

Pour half of sauce over noodles; stir to coat. Spread noodle mixture in shallow 1½-quart round or oval microproof dish.

Spread ½ teaspoon mustard on each ham slice. Roll up 3 asparagus spears in each ham slice. Place ham rolls, seam-side down, over noodles. Pour remaining sauce over ham. Sprinkle with paprika. Cook on HI 4 to 5 minutes, or until heated through. Let stand 2 minutes before serving.

Chicken and Rice Casserole _____ 4 to 6 servings

Total Cooking Time: 14 to 15 minutes

2 cups boned chicken, cut in 1-inch cubes
1 can (10¾ ounces) condensed cream of chicken soup
1 cup milk
1 cup sliced mushrooms
⅔ cup quick-cooking rice
1 envelope onion soup mix
¼ teaspoon poultry seasoning
½ cup shredded Cheddar cheese

Combine all ingredients, except cheese, in 1½-quart microproof casserole. Cover with plastic wrap. Cook on HI 14 to 15 minutes, stirring twice during cooking time. Sprinkle with cheese. Cover and let stand 10 minutes before serving.

← *Ham, Asparagus, and Noodle Casserole*

Cantonese Beef and Vegetables

4 to 5 servings

Total Cooking Time: 11 to 13 minutes

¼ **cup dry sherry**
¼ **cup soy sauce**
¼ **cup water**
1 **tablespoon sugar**
1 **clove garlic, minced**
1 **pound boneless beef steak, such as sirloin, thinly sliced**
6 **green onions**
1 **small head cauliflower**
1 **package (7 ounces) frozen pea pods**
1 **can (5 ounces) sliced water chestnuts, drained**

Combine sherry, soy sauce, water, sugar, and garlic in 2-quart glass dish. Add beef; stir. Cover with plastic wrap. Let stand, at room temperature, 4 hours, stirring occasionally.

Cut onions, white and green part, in 2-inch pieces; split lengthwise; set aside. Separate cauliflower into florets; slice each ¼-inch thick; set aside. Stir onions and cauliflower into beef mixture. Cover. Cook on HI 9 to 10 minutes, stirring once during cooking time. Stir in frozen pea pods and water chestnuts. Cover. Cook on HI 2 to 3 minutes, or until pea pods and cauliflower are crisp-tender. Serve over hot cooked rice.

Hearty Beef Vegetable Stew

6 to 8 servings

Total Cooking Time: 25 to 27 minutes

2¼ **cups water, divided**
2 **beef bouillon cubes**
1 **pound round steak, cut in ½-inch cubes**
3 **tablespoons cornstarch**
2 **large potatoes, peeled and cubed**
¾ **cup thinly sliced carrots**
½ **cup thinly sliced celery**
1 **medium onion, diced**
½ **teaspoon salt**
¼ **teaspoon freshly ground pepper**
¼ **teaspoon thyme**
1 **bay leaf, crushed**

Combine 2 cups of the water, bouillon cubes, and beef in 2-quart microproof bowl. Cook on HI 14 minutes, or until steak is tender. In 1-cup glass measure, mix remaining ¼ cup water and cornstarch. Add cornstarch and remaining ingredients to beef; stir. Cover with waxed paper. Cook on HI 11 to 13 minutes, or until vegetables are tender, stirring once. Cover and let stand 10 minutes before serving.

Ham and Potato Scallop ⎯⎯⎯⎯⎯⎯ 4 servings

Total Cooking Time: 17½ to 18½ minutes

1 **cup milk**	Pour milk into 2-cup glass measure.
2 **tablespoons butter or**	Cook on 70 for 2 minutes; set aside.
margarine	Place butter in 2-cup glass measure.
2 **tablespoons all-purpose**	Cook on HI 1 minute. Stir in flour.

1 **cup milk**
2 **tablespoons butter or margarine**
2 **tablespoons all-purpose flour**
1 **teaspoon prepared mustard**
½ **teaspoon salt**
¼ **teaspoon white pepper**
3 **medium potatoes, peeled and thinly sliced (about 1½ cups)**
1½ **cups cooked diced ham**
1 **teaspoon minced onion**
¼ **cup shredded Cheddar cheese**

Pour milk into 2-cup glass measure. Cook on 70 for 2 minutes; set aside. Place butter in 2-cup glass measure. Cook on HI 1 minute. Stir in flour. Cook on HI 30 seconds. Briskly stir hot milk, prepared mustard, salt, and pepper into butter. Set aside. Place potatoes in 1½-quart microproof casserole. Add ham and onion. Pour white sauce over ham and potatoes mixture; stir to combine. Cover with waxed paper. Cook on HI 14 to 15 minutes; stirring twice during cooking time. Sprinkle with cheese. Cover and let stand 10 minutes, or until cheese is melted.

Chicken and Spinach Casserole ⎯⎯⎯⎯⎯⎯⎯⎯⎯⎯ 4 servings

Total Cooking Time: 17 to 21 minutes

4 **tablespoons butter or margarine, divided**
½ **cup chopped onion**
2 **packages (10 ounces each) frozen chopped spinach, thawed and thoroughly drained**
2 **cups cooked diced chicken**
1 **can (10¾ ounces) condensed cream of chicken soup**
1 **cup shredded Swiss cheese**
3 **tablespoons chicken broth**
⅔ **cup fresh bread crumbs Paprika**

Combine 1 tablespoon butter with onion in 1-cup glass measure. Cook on HI 3 to 4 minutes, or until onion is tender. Stir onion into spinach. Spread mixture in 9-inch microproof baking dish. Spoon chicken evenly over spinach. Set aside. Combine soup, cheese, and broth in 4-cup glass measure. Cook on HI 3 minutes; stir to melt cheese. Pour evenly over chicken. Combine bread crumbs and remaining 3 tablespoons butter in 2-cup glass measure. Cook on HI 1 minute; stir to blend. Sprinkle bread crumbs on top. Sprinkle with paprika. Cook on HI 10 to 13 minutes, rotating dish midway through cooking time.

Ham Spaghetti Casserole ———— 6 to 8 servings

Total Cooking Time: 26 to 29 minutes

**4 slices bacon, cut into
1-inch pieces**
½ cup chopped onion
¼ cup chopped green pepper
**1 can (28 ounces) tomatoes,
broken up**
2 cups cooked cubed ham
1 cup broken thin spaghetti
½ teaspoon salt
½ teaspoon oregano
**⅛ teaspoon freshly ground
pepper**
**½ cup shredded Swiss
cheese**

Place bacon in 2-quart microproof casserole. Cover. Cook on HI 5 to 6 minutes, or until crisp; drain, reserving 2 tablespoons drippings in casserole. Add onion and green pepper. Cover. Cook on HI 5 minutes, or until onion is transparent. Add remaining ingredients, except cheese; stir and cover. Cook on HI 16 to 18 minutes, or until spaghetti is tender, stirring twice during cooking time. Stir. Sprinkle with cheese. Let stand until cheese is melted.

Tuna-Cashew Casserole ———— 5 to 6 servings

Total Cooking Time: 10 to 14 minutes

**1 can (10¾ ounces)
condensed cream of
mushroom soup**
¾ cup milk
3 cups cooked noodles
**1 can (6½ ounces) tuna,
drained and flaked**
½ cup diced celery
**½ cup broken salted cashew
nuts**
**1 tablespoon instant minced
onion**
½ teaspoon salt
**⅛ teaspoon freshly ground
pepper**
¼ cup crushed soda crackers

Blend soup and milk in 2-quart microproof casserole. Add remaining ingredients, except crackers; blend well. Cook on HI 8 to 10 minutes; stir. Top with cracker crumbs. Cook on HI 2 to 4 minutes, or until hot in center.

BUDGET-WISE MEAT

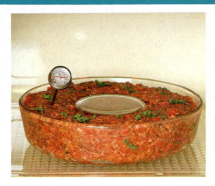

Arrangement is important when cooking meat (left). A microwave thermometer is helpful in determining preferred doneness for meat loaf (above).

Cooking meat in the microwave oven offers tremendous advantages. For best results, follow a recipe designed for microwave cooking. Since meat cooks so rapidly, care must be taken to avoid overcooking tender cuts of meat. When cooking pot roasts and less tender cuts which require long, moist cooking for the connective tissue to break down, you'll need only the proper understanding to achieve succulent results — with much less cooking time than conventional methods. Trimming the fat to allow the microwave energy to reach the meat itself is an important technique to follow. Also, the use of a browning agent, such as paprika, soy sauce, onion soup mix, tomato sauce, or a flavoring will enhance the recipe as well as give the meat a rich color.

As a tasty introduction to the pleasures of cooking meat in the microwave, be sure to try our Horseradish-Onion Beef Roast (page 108), Super Meat Loaf Ring (page 106), or Exotic Lamb Ragout (page 114).

Converting Your Recipes

Charts on the following pages outline microwave thawing and cooking times for the standard cuts of meat. For converting meat loaf, meat in sauces, and recipes that call for less tender cuts of meat, you're sure to find a similar recipe here to guide your own creations. Adapt your conventional recipes by matching ingredients and methods as closely as possible. Experiment as much as you like. Here are some helpful hints:

If you don't have a microproof ring mold, you can make one easily. Insert a small straight-sided glass, open end up, in the center of a round glass or microproof ceramic baking dish.

☐ Recipe times here presume meat is at refrigerator temperature. If your meal requires lengthy preparation during which the meat may reach room temperature, reduce cooking times.

☐ Less tender cuts of meat should be marinated or tenderized, and cooked at low power settings. With other cuts, baste, marinate, or season just as you would for conventional cooking.

☐ You can use a microwave roasting rack to elevate meat from its drippings during cooking.

☐ Check dishes that use relatively long cooking times to be sure liquid has not evaporated. Add liquid as necessary.

☐ Most ground beef recipes call for lean meat. If you use regular ground beef, drain fat before adding other ingredients.

The Defrosting Guide

1. Meat should be removed from its original packaging and placed in a microproof dish for defrosting. Remove all metal rings, wire twist ties, and all foil wrapping.

2. Defrost in the microwave oven only as long as necessary, since standing time will complete the thawing process.

3. Separate items like chops, bacon slices, and frankfurters as soon as possible. If pieces are not thawed, distribute them evenly in oven and continue defrosting.

4. Slightly increase the time for weights larger than on the chart. Do not double.

DEFROSTING GUIDE — MEAT

Meat	Amount	Power Control Setting	Time (minutes per pound)	Standing Time (minutes)	Special Notes
Beef					
Ground beef		30	5 - 6	5	Turn over once. Remove thawed portions with fork. Return remainder. Freeze in doughnut shape. Depress center when freezing. Defrost on plate.
	¼-lb. patty	30	1 per patty	2	
Pot roast, chuck	under 4 lbs.	30	3 - 5	10	Turn over once.
	over 4 lbs.	70	3 - 5	10	Turn over once.
Rib roast, rolled	2 to 4 lbs.	30	6 - 8	30 - 45	Turn over once.
	6 to 8 lbs.	70	6 - 8	90	Turn over twice.
Rib roast, bone in		70	5 - 6	45 - 90	Turn over twice.
Rump roast	3 to 4 lbs.	30	3 - 5	30	Turn over once.
	6 to 7 lbs.	70	3 - 5	45	Turn over twice.
Round steak		30	4 - 5	5 - 10	Turn over once.
Flank steak		30	4 - 5	5 - 10	Turn over once.
Sirloin steak	½" thick	30	4 - 5	5 - 10	Turn over once.
Tenderloin steaks	2 to 3 lbs.	30	4 - 5	8 - 10	Turn over once.
Stew beef	2 lbs.	30	3 - 5	8 - 10	Turn over once. Separate.
Lamb					
Cubed for stew		30	7 - 8	5	Turn over once. Separate.
Ground lamb	under 4 lbs.	30	3 - 5	30 - 45	Turn over once.
	over 4 lbs.	70	3 - 5	30 - 45	Turn over twice.
Chops	1" thick	30	5 - 8	15	Turn over twice.
Leg	5 - 8 lbs.	30	4 - 5	15 - 20	Turn over twice.
Pork					
Chops	½" thick	30	4 - 6	5 - 10	Separate chops halfway through defrosting time.
	1" thick	30	5 - 7	10	
Spareribs, country-style ribs		30	5 - 7	10	Turn over once.
Roast	under 4 lbs.	30	4 - 5	30 - 45	Turn over once.
	over 4 lbs.	70	4 - 5	30 - 45	Turn over twice.
Bacon	1 lb.	30	2 - 3	3 - 5	Defrost until strips separate.
Sausage, bulk	1 lb.	30	2 - 3	3 - 5	Turn over once. Remove thawed portions with fork. Return remainder.
Sausage links	1 lb.	30	3 - 5	4 - 6	Turn over once. Defrost until pieces can be separated.
Hot dogs		30	5 - 6	5	
Veal					
Roast	3 to 4 lbs.	30	5 - 7	30	Turn over once.
	6 to 7 lbs.	70	5 - 7	90	Turn over twice.
Chops	½" thick	30	4 - 6	20	Turn over once. Separate chops and continue defrosting.
Variety Meat					
Liver		30	5 - 6	10	Turn over once.
Tongue		30	7 - 8	10	Turn over once.

Using the Cooking Guide

1. Meat should be completely thawed before cooking.
2. Place meat, fat-side down, on microwave roasting rack set in microproof baking dish.
3. Meat may be covered lightly with waxed paper to stop splatters.
4. Use a microwave thermometer for the most accurate cooking of larger cuts of meat. Insert thermometer as horizontally as possible, avoiding fat and bone.

5. Unless otherwise noted, times given for steaks and patties will give medium doneness.
6. During standing time, the internal temperature of roasts will rise between 5°F and 15°F. Hence, standing time is considered an essential part of the time required to complete cooking.
7. Breaded cutlets and chops are cooked in the same time as that shown on chart.

COOKING GUIDE — MEAT

Meat	First Power Control Setting And Time	Second Power Control Setting And Time	Standing Time (minutes)	Special Notes
Beef Ground beef Bulk	HI 2½ minutes per pound	Stir. HI 2½ minutes per pound	5	Crumble in microproof dish, cook covered.
Ground beef patty, 4 oz., ½" thick	HI 1 minute	Turn over. HI 1 - 1½ minutes		Preheat browning dish according to manufacturer's directions.
2	HI 1 - 1½ minutes	Turn over. HI 1 - 1½ minutes		Preheat browning dish according to manufacturer's directions.
4	HI 3 minutes	Turn over. HI 3 - 3½ minutes		Preheat browning dish according to manufacturer's directions.
Meat loaf 1½ - 2 lbs.	HI 12 - 14 minutes	None	5 - 10	Microproof loaf dish or microproof ring mold.
Beef rib roast, boneless	HI Rare: 4 - 5 minutes per pound Medium: 5 - 6 minutes per pound Well: 6 - 7 minutes per pound	Turn over. 70 3 - 4 minutes per pound 5 - 6 minutes per pound 6 - 7 minutes per pound	10 10 10	Microproof dish with microwave roasting rack.

Meat	First Power Control Setting And Time	Second Power Control Setting And Time	Standing Time (minutes)	Special Notes
Rib roast, bone in	HI Rare: 3 - 4 minutes per pound Medium: 4 - 5 minutes per pound Well: 5 - 6 minutes per pound	Turn over. 70 3 - 4 minutes per pound 3 - 5 minutes per pound 5 - 6 minutes per pound	10	Microproof dish with microwave roasting rack.
Beef pot roast, boneless	HI 5 minutes per pound	Turn over. 50 20 minutes per pound	10 - 15	Covered micro-proof casserole or cooking bag. Requires liquid.
Beef brisket, boneless, fresh or corned 2½ - 3½ lbs.	HI 5 minutes per pound	Turn over. 50 20 minutes per pound	10 - 15	4-quart micro-proof casserole with tight cover. Water to cover.
Top round steak	HI 5 minutes per pound	Turn over. 50 5 minutes per pound	10 - 15	Microproof casse-role with tight cover. Requires liquid.
Sirloin steak ¾ - 1" thick	HI 4½ minutes per pound	Drain dish and turn over. HI 2 minutes per pound	10 - 15	*
Minute steak or cube steak 4 - 6 oz. steaks	HI 1 - 2 minutes	Drain dish and turn over. HI 1 - 2 minutes		*
Tenderloin 4 - 8 oz. 1-inch thick	HI Rare: 5 minutes Med: 6 minutes Well: 9 minutes	Drain, turn steak HI 1 - 2 minutes 2 - 3 minutes 2 - 3 minutes	10 - 15	*
Rib eye or strip steak ½ - 2 lbs.	HI Rare: 4 minutes Med: 5 minutes Well: 7 minutes	Turn over. HI ½ - 1 minute 1 - 2 minutes 2 - 3 minutes	5 - 10	*
Lamb				
Ground lamb patties 1 - 2 lbs.	HI 4 minutes	Turn over. HI 4 - 5 minutes	5 - 10	*
Lamb chops 1 - 1½ lbs., 1" thick	HI 8 minutes	Turn over. HI 7 - 8 minutes	5 - 10	*
Lamb leg or shoulder roast, bone in	70 Medium: 4 - 5 minutes per pound Well: 5 - 6 minutes per pound	Cover end of leg bone with foil. Turn over. 70 Medium: 4 - 5 minutes per pound Well: 5 - 6 minutes per pound	5 10	In microproof dish with microwave roasting rack.

*Shallow microproof baking dish or browning dish preheated according to manufacturer's directions.

Meat	First Power Control Setting And Time	Second Power Control Setting And Time	Standing Time (minutes)	Special Notes
Lamb roast, boneless	70 5 - 6 minutes per pound	Turn over. 70 5 - 6 minutes per pound	5 to 10	In shallow microproof baking dish with microwave roasting rack.
Veal				
Shoulder or rump roast, boneless 2 - 3½ lbs.	70 9 minutes per pound	Turn over. 70 9 - 10 minutes per pound	5 to 10	In shallow microproof baking dish with microwave roasting rack.
Veal cutlets or loin chops ½" thick	HI 2 minutes per pound	Turn over HI 2 - 3½ minutes per pound		*
Pork				
Pork chops ½ - ¾" thick	HI 6 minutes per pound	Turn over. HI 5 - 6 minutes per pound	5	*
Spareribs	70 6 - 7 minutes per pound	Turn over. 70 6 - 7 minutes per pound	10	Begin in liquid in 3-quart casserole and transfer to microproof baking dish to finish.
Pork loin roast, boneless 3 - 5 lbs.	HI 6 minutes per pound	Turn over. 70 5 - 6 minutes per pound	10	Microproof baking dish.
Pork loin, center cut 4 - 5 lbs.	HI 5 - 6 minutes per pound	Turn over. 70 4 - 5 minutes per pound	10	Microproof baking dish.
Ham, boneless, precooked	70 5 - 7 minutes per pound	Turn over. 70 5 - 7 minutes per pound	10	In shallow microproof dish with microwave roasting rack.
Center cut ham slice precooked 1 - 1½ lbs.	70 5 minutes per pound	Turn over. 70 5 - 6 minutes per pound	5	Shallow microproof baking dish.
Smoked ham shank	70 4 - 5 minutes per pound	Turn over. 70 4 - 5 minutes per pound	10	In shallow microproof baking dish with microwave roasting rack.
Canned ham 3 lbs.	70 5 - 6 minutes per pound	70 5 - 6 minutes per pound	10	In shallow microproof baking dish with microwave roasting rack.
5 lbs.	70 4 - 5 minutes per pound	Turn over. 70 4 - 5 minutes per pound	10	In shallow microproof baking dish with microwave roasting rack.
Sausage patties ½ - ¾" thick	HI 2 minutes	Turn over. HI 1½ - 2 minutes per pound		*
Sausage, bulk 1 lb.	HI 3 minutes	Stir. HI 1 - 2 minutes		Crumble into 1½-quart microproof dish, covered.

Shallow microproof baking dish or browning dish preheated according to manufacturer's directions.

Meat	First Power Control Setting And Time	Second Power Control Setting And Time	Standing Time (minutes)	Special Notes
Pork sausage links ½ lb. 1 lb.	Pierce casing HI 1 minute HI 2 minutes	Turn over. HI 1 - 1½ minutes HI 1½ - 2 minutes		*
Bratwurst, precooked	Pierce casing 70 5 minutes per pound	Rearrange. 70 4 - 5 minutes per pound		*
Polish sausage, knockwurst, ring bologna	Pierce casing 80 2 - 2½ minutes per pound	Rearrange 80 2 - 2½ minutes per pound		*
Hot dogs 1 2 4	80 25 - 30 seconds 80 25 - 40 seconds 80 50 - 55 seconds			Shallow microproof dish. Shallow microproof dish. Shallow microproof dish.
Bacon 1 slice 2 slices 4 slices 6 slices 8 slices	HI 45 sec. - 1 min. HI 2 - 2½ minutes HI 4 - 4½ minutes HI 5 - 6 minutes HI 6 - 7 minutes			On paper towel-lined dish or microwave roasting rack covered with paper towel with edges tucked under rack or dish.

* *Shallow microproof baking dish or browning dish preheated according to manufacturer's directions.*

REHEATING GUIDE — CONVENIENCE BEEF

Food	Amount	Power Control Setting	Time (minutes)	Special Notes
Barbecued beef, chili, stew, hash, meatballs, etc.	16 oz. (can) or less	80	3 - 5	Remove from cans to microproof plate or casserole, cover. Stir halfway through cooking time.
Stuffed peppers, cabbage rolls, chow mein, etc.	16 - 32 oz. (can)	80	5 - 9	
Barbecued beef, chili, stew, corned beef hash, meatballs, patties in sauce, gravy	8 - 16 oz. package (frozen)	HI	5 - 11	Remove from foil container to microproof casserole, cover. Slit plastic pouches.
Dry casserole mixes, cooked hamburger added	6½ - 8 oz. package	HI	18 - 22	Remove mix from package to 3-quart microproof casserole. Cover. Stir once.

Super Meat Loaf Ring _____ 6 to 8 servings

Total Cooking Time: 14½ to 16½ minutes

2 **pounds lean ground beef**
2 **eggs, lightly beaten**
2 **slices fresh white bread, crumbled**
1 **envelope onion soup mix**
2 **tablespoons milk**
1 **teaspoon prepared mustard**
1 **tablespoon minced fresh parsley**
1 **can (8 ounces) tomato sauce, divided**

Topping
1 **tablespoon brown sugar**
1 **tablespoon vinegar**

Combine all ingredients, except tomato sauce and topping ingredients, in large bowl. Add ¼ cup tomato sauce to meat mixture; mix thoroughly. Spoon into 4- or 5-cup microproof ring mold. Cook on HI 13 to 15 minutes, rotating every 10 minutes. Meat loaf ring is done when it pulls away from side of mold. Let stand 5 minutes; drain. Invert onto warmed serving platter.

To prepare Topping, mix sugar, remaining tomato sauce, and vinegar in 2-cup glass measure. Cook on HI 1½ minutes. Stir. Pour half the sauce over meat loaf ring. Serve remaining sauce as gravy.

Country Meatballs _____ 4 servings

Total Cooking Time: 11½ to 13½ minutes

¾ **pound lean ground beef**
1 **egg, lightly beaten**
¼ **teaspoon garlic powder**
¼ **cup tomato juice**
¼ **cup dry bread crumbs**
1 **cup milk**
2 **tablespoons butter or margarine**
2 **tablespoons all-purpose flour**
2 **teaspoons instant minced onion**
½ **teaspoon Worcestershire sauce**
½ **teaspoon salt**
¼ **teaspoon freshly ground pepper**

Combine beef, egg, garlic powder, tomato juice, and bread crumbs in mixing bowl; blend well. Shape into 16 meatballs. Place in 1½-quart microproof casserole. Cover with waxed paper. Cook on HI 5 minutes; drain; set aside. Pour milk into 2-cup glass measure. Cook on 70 for 2 minutes; set aside.

Melt butter on HI 30 seconds in another 2-cup glass measure. Stir in flour. Cook on HI 1 minute. Briskly stir in warm milk. Add remaining ingredients; mix lightly. Pour over meatballs. Cover with waxed paper. Cook on HI 3 to 5 minutes, or until beef is no longer red and sauce is thickened. Serve over cooked noodles or rice, if desired.

Spicy Stuffed Peppers

4 servings

Total Cooking Time: 18 to 20 minutes

4 **large green peppers, tops removed and seeded**
¾ **pound lean ground beef**
1 **cup quick-cooking rice**
¼ **cup finely chopped onion**
½ **teaspoon salt**
¼ **teaspoon freshly ground pepper**
¼ **teaspoon garlic powder**
1 **can (8 ounces) tomato sauce**
5 **slices sharp Cheddar cheese**

Arrange peppers in 8-cup microproof ring mold or 10-inch microproof pie plate. Combine remaining ingredients, except tomato sauce and cheese; blend thoroughly. Divide meat mixture among peppers. Pour tomato sauce over peppers. Cover with plastic wrap. Cook on HI 18 to 20 minutes, or until peppers are tender and beef is no longer red. Remove plastic wrap; top each pepper with cheese slice. Return plastic wrap. Let stand 10 minutes before serving.

Barbecued Chuck Roast

6 to 8 servings

Total Cooking Time: 60 to 65 minutes

1 **cup barbecue sauce**
½ **cup chopped onion**
1 **clove garlic, minced**
1 **tablespoon all-purpose flour**
1 **tablespoon beef bouillon granules**
3 **pounds boneless beef chuck roast**

Cut 1-inch strip from open end of cooking bag; set aside. Combine barbecue sauce, onion, garlic, flour, and bouillon. Place roast in bag. Spoon sauce mixture evenly over roast. Secure bag with reserved strip. Place bag in an 12 × 7-inch microproof baking dish. Cook on 30 for 30 minutes; turn bag over. Cook on 30 for 30 to 35 minutes.

Make barbecued beef sandwiches with leftover roast beef by shredding it, mixing with enough sauce to moisten, and heating in buns.

Horseradish-Onion Beef Roast —— 6 to 8 servings

Total Cooking Time: 15 to 19 minutes

1 boneless beef round rump roast (3 to 3½ pounds)
1 clove garlic, minced
½ cup prepared horseradish
1 tablespoon steak sauce
1 envelope (1½ ounces) onion soup mix, divided
2 tablespoons all-purpose flour
¼ cup cold water
½ teaspoon salt
Dash freshly ground pepper

Remove string from roast, if tied. Cut roast almost in half horizontally. Gently open roast. Thoroughly slash inside of roast; do not cut all the way through. Combine garlic, horseradish, and steak sauce in small bowl. Spread mixture over cut surface of roast. Press roast together; tie securely with string. Place in shallow 2½ to 3-quart microproof baking dish. Sprinkle top with half of the onion soup mix. Cover with waxed paper. Cook on HI 5 minutes.

Cook on 70 for 7 to 10 minutes. Place roast on warm serving platter. Cover with foil to keep warm while preparing gravy. (Internal temperature of roast will rise to 140°F, medium rare.)

Pour drippings into 4-cup glass measure; skim fat. Add enough water to equal 1 cup. Combine flour, remaining onion soup mix, and ¼ cup cold water in small bowl; blend well. Stir into drippings. Cook on HI 3 to 4 minutes, or until thickened, stirring at one minute intervals. Stir in salt and pepper. Serve hot with sliced roast.

Leftover Meat Stew ——————— 5 to 6 servings

Total Cooking Time: 28 to 30 minutes

**2 to 3 cups cooked cubed
   beef, pork, or lamb**
**4 medium carrots, peeled
   and sliced**
**3 medium potatoes, peeled
   and cubed**
1 medium onion, quartered
1 cup water
**1 package (¾ ounce)
   mushroom gravy mix**
**1 teaspoon Worcestershire
   sauce**
1 teaspoon salt
**⅛ teaspoon freshly ground
   pepper**
**1 cup fresh or frozen peas
   Minced fresh parsley**

Combine all ingredients, except peas and parsley, in 3-quart microproof casserole. Cover. Cook on HI 25 to 27 minutes, or until vegetables are tender, stirring every 10 minutes. Stir in peas. Cover. Cook on 50 for 3 minutes. Sprinkle with parsley. Let stand 5 minutes before serving.

Baked Ham Classic ——————— 8 to 12 servings

Total Cooking Time: 26 to 29 minutes

**1 canned ham (3 pounds)
   Whole cloves**
3 tablespoons brown sugar
**2 tablespoons apple or
   orange juice**
1 tablespoon cornstarch
1 teaspoon dry mustard

Place ham on microwave baking rack in microproof baking dish. Cover with waxed paper. Cook on 70 for 10 minutes. Turn ham over. Score top in diamond pattern. Insert clove in center of each diamond. Combine sugar, juice, cornstarch, and mustard in 2-cup glass measure. Cook on HI 1 minute, or until thickened. Brush half of glaze over ham. Cook on 70 for 15 to 18 minutes. Reglaze ham after 5 minutes. Let stand, covered with foil, for 15 minutes before serving.

Honey-Glazed Pork Roast _____ 6 to 8 servings

Total Cooking Time: 24 to 28 minutes

¼ **cup honey**
2 **tablespoons orange juice**
¾ **teaspoon cinnamon**
1 **teaspoon cornstarch**
1 **rolled boneless pork loin roast (3 to 3½ pounds)**

Combine honey, orange juice, cinnamon, and cornstarch in 2-cup glass measure. Cook on HI 1 minute, or until glaze boils and thickens; set aside.

Place roast, fat-side down, on microwave roasting rack in shallow glass baking dish. Cover with plastic wrap. Cook on 70 for 10 minutes. Turn roast over. Cover with waxed paper and cook on 70 for 12 to 15 minutes. Brush on half of the glaze. Cook, uncovered, on 70 for 1 to 2 minutes, or until glaze is bubbly. Brush with remaining glaze. Let stand 10 minutes before serving.

Ribs with Dill and Tomato _____ 4 servings

Total Cooking Time: 36 to 38 minutes

2½ **pounds pork spareribs, cut into serving pieces**
1 **can (12 ounces) tomato paste**
½ **cup water**
¼ **cup chopped green pepper**
¼ **cup minced onion**
½ **teaspoon salt**
¼ **teaspoon freshly ground pepper**
¼ **teaspoon dillweed**

Arrange ribs in 8-inch square microproof dish. Combine remaining ingredients in small bowl; blend well; pour over ribs. Cover with waxed paper. Cook on 70 for 36 to 38 minutes, or until tender and no longer pink. Turn ribs over and rearrange midway through cooking time. Let stand 10 minutes before serving.

Honey-Glazed Pork Roast   ➧

Sauced Pork Chops ———————— 4 servings
Total Cooking Time: 18 to 21 minutes

4 **center loin pork chops**
    (about ¾-inch thick)
¼ **teaspoon salt**
¼ **teaspoon freshly ground**
    pepper
1 **can (11 ounces) mandarin**
    oranges, drained,
    liquid reserved
½ **cup chopped chutney**
2 **tablespoons lemon juice**
1 **tablespoon sugar**
1 **tablespoon cornstarch**

Arrange pork chops in 8-inch round microproof baking dish, placing thickest portions toward outside of dish. Sprinkle with salt and pepper. Cover with waxed paper. Cook on HI 10 minutes; drain; turn chops over. Mix ⅓ cup reserved orange liquid with chutney, lemon juice, and sugar. Arrange orange sections over pork chops. Top with chutney mixture. Cover. Cook on HI 6 to 8 minutes, or until thoroughly done. Remove chops to warmed serving platter. Cover to keep warm.

Mix cornstarch and 2 tablespoons orange liquid. Stir into juices in dish. Cook on HI 2 to 3 minutes, or until thickened and smooth, stirring twice during cooking. Spoon over chops.

Smothered Ham Steak ———————— 6 servings
Total Cooking Time: 19 to 21 minutes

1 **tablespoon vegetable oil**
2 **cups chopped onions**
1 **large green pepper,**
    seeded and cut into
    ¼-inch rings
1 **can (8 ounces) tomato**
    sauce
1 **tablespoon cornstarch**
½ **teaspoon dry mustard**
⅛ **teaspoon ground cloves**
1 **to 1½ pounds sliced,**
    precooked ham,
    trimmed

Combine oil, onions, and green pepper in 2-quart glass measure. Cook on 90 for 12 minutes, or until vegetables are tender, stirring once during cooking time. Combine tomato sauce, cornstarch, mustard, and cloves in small bowl; stir until cornstarch is dissolved. Add to onion mixture.

Place ham in shallow 1½-quart microproof dish. (Ham must lie flat.) Pour tomato mixture over ham. Cook on HI 7 to 9 minutes, or until sauce is thickened and ham is hot. Let stand, covered, 5 minutes before serving.

Veal-Caraway Stew _____ 4 servings

Total Cooking Time: 40 to 44 minutes

1 **pound boneless veal, cut into 1-inch cubes**
1 **package (1½ ounces) brown gravy mix**
1 **cup chicken broth**
1 **teaspoon salt**
⅛ **teaspoon freshly ground pepper**
2 **tablespoons minced onion**
2 **stalks celery, sliced**
2 **medium carrots, thinly sliced**
2 **teaspoons caraway seed**
Hot cooked noodles or spaetzle

Combine veal, gravy mix, and chicken broth in 3-quart microproof casserole. Cover. Cook on 70 for 10 minutes, stirring once during cooking time. Add remaining ingredients, except noodles; blend well. Cover. Cook on 50 for 30 to 34 minutes, or until meat and vegetables are tender, stirring once during cooking time. Let stand 5 minutes before serving with noodles or spaetzle.

A combination of ½ pound pork and ½ pound veal can be substituted for all veal.

Veal Parmigiana _____ 4 servings

Total Cooking Time: 14 to 15 minutes

4 **veal cutlets (¼ pound each)**
1 **medium egg**
¼ **teaspoon salt**
⅓ **cup grated Parmesan cheese**
3 **tablespoons cracker crumbs**
2 **tablespoons vegetable oil**
¼ **cup dry vermouth**
1 **medium onion, minced**
1 **cup (4 ounces) shredded mozzarella cheese**
1 **can (6 ounces) tomato paste**
⅛ **teaspoon freshly ground pepper**
⅛ **teaspoon oregano**

Place each veal cutlet between 2 sheets of waxed paper. Pound with smooth-surfaced meat mallet until veal is ¼-inch thick; set aside. Beat egg and salt in shallow dish. Combine Parmesan cheese and cracker crumbs on sheet of waxed paper. Dip veal in egg mixture, then in crumb mixture; set aside. Preheat microwave browning dish according to manufacturer's directions. Pour oil into browning dish. Place cutlets on browning dish. Cover loosely with waxed paper. Cook on HI 3 minutes, turning over once during cooking time. Pour vermouth over veal. Sprinkle with onion. Top with mozzarella cheese and tomato paste. Sprinkle with pepper and oregano. Cover. Cook on 60 for 6 minutes.

Exotic Lamb Ragout ———————— 4 servings

Total Cooking Time: 36½ to 42½ minutes

1 tablespoon vegetable oil
1 cup chopped onions
1 pound boneless lamb, cut into 1-inch cubes
1 package (1½ ounces) brown gravy mix
2 cups chicken broth, divided
1 teaspoon salt
⅛ teaspoon freshly ground pepper
½ teaspoon nutmeg
½ cup raisins
½ cup long-grain rice
1 tablespoon lemon juice
1 tablespoon butter or margarine
½ cup blanched slivered almonds

Combine oil and onions in 3-quart microproof casserole. Cook on 90 for 3 minutes. Add lamb, gravy mix, and 1 cup of the chicken broth. Cook on HI 5 minutes. Stir in salt, pepper, nutmeg, raisins, rice, remaining 1 cup broth, and lemon juice. Cover. Cook on 50 for 25 to 30 minutes, or until rice and lamb are tender, stirring every 10 minutes. Add small amount of water if mixture becomes dry. Set aside. Place butter in 8-inch glass pie plate. Cook on HI 30 seconds, or until melted. Stir in almonds. Cover with waxed paper. Cook on HI 3 to 4 minutes, or until almonds are golden, stirring twice during cooking time. Sprinkle almonds over lamb and serve.

Braised Lamb Shanks ———————— 2 servings

Total Cooking Time: 18 to 20 minutes

2 lamb shanks
1 can (10½ ounces) beef broth
½ teaspoon onion flakes
1 clove garlic, minced
¼ teaspoon freshly ground pepper
1 bay leaf

Place lamb shanks in 2-quart microproof casserole. Combine remaining ingredients; blend well; pour over lamb. Cover with plastic wrap. Cook on 30 for 10 minutes. Turn lamb over. Cover. Cook on HI 8 to 10 minutes, or until lamb is no longer pink. Discard bay leaf. Let stand 5 minutes before serving.

POULTRY PLATTERS

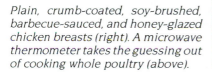

Plain, crumb-coated, soy-brushed, barbecue-sauced, and honey-glazed chicken breasts (right). A microwave thermometer takes the guessing out of cooking whole poultry (above).

Still about our most economical food, chicken is more juicy, flavorful, and tender than ever when cooked in the microwave oven. It is a special favorite of microwave cooks because it requires less attention than most main dish meat. Duck, Cornish hen, and turkey parts are great, too.

Poultry turns out golden brown, though not dark brown or crisp. If you are a crisp-skin lover, the microwave oven is still for you.

Simply crisp the skin in a conventional oven at 450°F for 5 or 10 minutes following the microwave cooking time. And how about this time-saving twist for charcoal grilling: you can avoid the long time delays by partially cooking poultry in the microwave oven, then finishing it on the grill! Full charcoal-grilled flavor is retained. Try the tasty recipes suggested here, then adapt your own favorites.

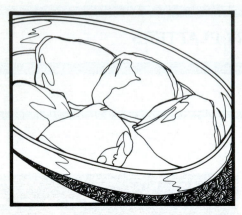

Arrange chicken pieces with thickest portions along edge of dish.

Converting Your Recipes

Conventional one-dish poultry recipes that call for cut-up pieces are easy to adapt for the microwave oven. You are sure to find a similar recipe in this chapter to use as a guide. Here, too, are some tips to follow:

☐ Use care in selecting whole poultry. Chances are your oven will not be able to manage a whole turkey. (Even the largest microwave ovens cannot accommodate a turkey larger than 12 to 14 pounds).

☐ Conventional pop-up indicators for doneness do not work correctly in the microwave oven.

☐ When using a microwave thermometer, insert it in the fleshy part of the inside thigh muscle, without touching the bone.

☐ Standing time is essential to complete cooking. Depending upon size, allow up to 15 minutes standing time for whole poultry. The internal temperature will rise approximately 15°F during 15 minutes standing time. Chicken pieces and casseroles need only 5 minutes standing time.

The Defrosting Guide

1. Poultry should be removed from its original packaging and placed in a microproof dish for defrosting. Remove all metal rings, wire twist ties, and any aluminum foil. Metal leg clamps, which are difficult to remove, need not be removed until after defrosting. Be careful, of course, that the metal is at least 1 inch from the oven walls.

2. Defrost only as long as necessary. Poultry should be cool in the center when removed from the oven.

3. To speed defrosting during standing time, poultry may be placed in cold water.

4. Separate chicken pieces as soon as partially thawed.

5. Wing and leg tips and area near breastbone may begin cooking before center is thoroughly defrosted. When these areas appear thawed, cover them with small strips of aluminum foil; keep this foil at least 1 inch from oven walls.

DEFROSTING GUIDE — POULTRY

Food	Amount	Minutes (per pound)	Power Control Setting	Standing Time (minutes)	Special Notes
Capon	6 - 8 lbs.	2	70	60	Turn over once. Immerse in cold water for standing time.
Chicken, cut up	2 - 3 lbs.	5 - 6	30	10 - 15	Turn over once. Separate pieces when partially thawed.
Chicken, whole	2 - 3 lbs.	6 - 8	30	25 - 30	Turn over once. Immerse in cold water for standing time.
Cornish hens	1, 1 - 1½ lbs. 2, 1 - 1½ lbs. each	12 - 13 20 - 21	30 30	20 20	Turn over once.
Duckling	4 - 5 lbs.	4	70	30 - 40	Turn over once. Immerse in cold water for standing time.
Turkey breast	Under 4 lbs. Over 4 lbs.	3 - 5 1 2	30 70 30	20 20	Turn over once. Start at 70, turn over, continue on 30.
Turkey parts	1 - 2 lbs.	5 - 6	30	15 - 20	Turn every 5 minutes. Separate pieces when partially thawed.
Turkey roast, boneless	2 - 4 lbs.	3 - 4	30	10	Remove from foil pan. Cover with waxed paper.

Using the Cooking Guide

1. Defrost frozen poultry completely before cooking.
2. Remove giblets and rinse poultry in cool water; then pat dry.
3. When cooking whole birds, place on a microwave roasting rack in a microproof baking dish large enough to catch drippings.
4. Turn over, as directed in Guide, halfway through cooking time.
5. Cook whole poultry covered loosely with a waxed paper tent to prevent splattering. Toward end of cooking time, small pieces of aluminum foil may be used to cover legs, wing tips, or breastbone area to prevent overcooking. Keep foil at least 1 inch from oven walls.
6. Cover poultry pieces with microproof casserole lid or plastic wrap during cooking.
7. Standing time completes the cooking of poultry. Cooked whole birds may be covered with aluminum foil during standing time.

COOKING GUIDE — POULTRY

Food	First Power Control Setting And Time	Second Power Control Setting And Time	Standing Time (minutes)	Special Notes
Chicken, whole 2 - 3 pounds 3 - 5 pounds	HI 3 - 4 per pound HI 4 per pound	Turn over. HI 4 per pound Turn over. HI 4 - 5 per pound	5 (covered with foil) 5	In shallow micro- proof baking dish with microwave roasting rack, breast-side up.
Chicken, cut up 2½-3½ pounds	HI 10	Turn over. HI 8 - 12	5	Microproof baking dish. Cover.
Chicken, quartered	HI 3 - 4 per pound	Turn over. HI 3 - 4 per pound	5	Shallow microproof baking dish, skin- side down.
Cornish hens 1 - 1½ pounds	HI 4 per pound	Turn over. HI 3 per pound	5	In shallow micro- proof baking dish with microwave roasting rack. Breast-side down. Cover.
Duckling 4 - 5 pounds	70 4 per pound	Turn over. Drain excess fat. 70 4 per pound	8 - 10	In shallow micro- proof baking dish with microwave roasting rack. Cover.
Turkey breast 3 - 4 pounds	HI 7 per pound	Turn over. 70 5 per pound		Shallow microproof baking dish.
Turkey roast, boneless 2 - 4 pounds	70 10 per pound	Turn over. 70 9 per pound	10 - 15	Microproof loaf pan. Cover with plastic wrap.
Turkey parts 2 - 3 pounds	70 7 - 8 per pound	Turn over. 70 7 - 8 per pound	5	In shallow micro- proof baking dish with microwave roasting rack.

REHEATING GUIDE — CONVENIENCE POULTRY

Food	Amount	Power Control Setting	Time (minutes)	Special Notes
Chicken, frozen fried	1½ - 2 lbs.			Follow package directions. Remove wrapping and place in shallow microproof baking dish.
Chicken Kiev, frozen	1 - 2 pieces			Follow package directions. Remove plastic wrap, place on microproof plate.
Chicken à la King, frozen	5 oz.	HI	3 - 4	Place on microproof plate. Stir before serving.
Creamed Chicken, Chicken and Dumplings, canned	10½ oz.	80	2 - 4	Stir once.
Chicken chow mein, canned	14 - 24 oz.	80	4 - 6	Place in shallow microproof baking dish. Stir halfway through cooking time.
Turkey tetrazzini, frozen	12 oz.	HI	3 - 4	Place on microproof plate. Stir before serving.
Turkey, sliced in gravy, frozen	5 oz.	HI	3 - 5	Place in microproof dish. Make slit in pouch before heating.

Oven Baked Chicken _____ 4 to 6 servings

Total Cooking Time: 24 to 27 minutes

2½- to 3-pound frying chicken, cut up
⅓ cup sherry
1 envelope (2⅜ ounces) seasoned coating mix for chicken

Wash chicken and pat dry with paper towels. Dip in sherry. Place seasoned coating mix in plastic bag. Shake a few pieces of chicken at a time until coated. Arrange in 10-inch round microproof dish, skin-side up, with thickest portions toward outside of dish. Cover with paper towels. Cook on HI 24 to 27 minutes, or until chicken is tender. Let stand 5 minutes before serving.

For crisper and browner chicken, do not cover. If splattering occurs, cover lightly with paper towels.

To reduce calories, substitute chicken bouillon for sherry.

Chicken Tetrazzini ———————————— 4 to 6 servings
Total Cooking Time: 11 to 14 minutes

**2 ounces uncooked
    spaghetti, broken
    into 2-inch
    pieces
1 tablespoon butter or
    margarine
⅓ cup minced onion
¼ pound mushrooms, sliced
1½ tablespoons all-purpose
    flour
1 cup chicken broth
¼ cup light cream or
    half-and-half
⅛ cup dry vermouth
½ cup grated Parmesan
    cheese, divided
¼ teaspoon salt
    Dash white pepper
1 cup diced cooked chicken
1 tablespoon minced fresh
    parsley**

Cook spaghetti according to package
directions. Drain immediately; rinse in
cold water to stop cooking; set aside.
Place butter, onion, and mushrooms in
1½-quart microproof casserole. Cover.
Cook on HI 2 to 3 minutes, or until
onion is transparent. Stir in flour to
make a paste.

Combine broth, cream, and vermouth
in 4-cup glass measure. Cook on HI 2
minutes; slowly stir into flour mixture;
blend thoroughly. Stir in ¼ cup cheese,
salt, and pepper; blend well. Cook on
HI 5 to 7 minutes, or until mixture
comes to a boil and thickens, stirring
once during cooking time.

Carefully stir in cooked spaghetti,
chicken, and remaining cheese. Cover.
Cook on HI 2 minutes. Let stand,
covered, 5 minutes before serving.
Sprinkle with parsley.

Chicken Stroganoff ———————————— 6 servings
Total Cooking Time: 23 to 26 minutes

**1 large onion, chopped
1 tablespoon vegetable oil
1 tablespoon prepared
    mustard
1 can (8 ounces) tomato
    sauce
1 can (4 ounces) mushroom
    pieces, drained
3 whole chicken breasts,
    halved, skinned, and
    boned
½ cup dairy sour cream
2 tablespoons minced fresh
    parsley**

Combine onion and oil in 4-cup glass
measure. Cook on 90 for 5 minutes, or
until onion is transparent. Stir in mustard, tomato sauce, and mushrooms;
set aside

Place chicken in shallow 1½-quart
microproof casserole; spoon tomato
sauce over chicken. Cover with plastic
wrap. Cook on HI 16 to 18 minutes, or
until chicken is done, turning chicken
over halfway through cooking time.
Use slotted spoon to remove chicken
to a warmed serving platter. Stir sour
cream into tomato sauce. Cook on 50
for 2 to 3 minutes, or until hot. Pour
over chicken and sprinkle with parsley.
Serve with noodles or rice, if desired.

Chicken Veronique ———————— 4 to 6 servings

Total Cooking Time: 11 to 14 minutes

**3 cups cooked long-grain
    rice**
**2 cups cubed cooked
    chicken**
**1 cup seedless green or
    white grapes, halved**
½ cup diced celery
¾ cup milk
¼ cup white wine, optional
**2 tablespoons butter or
    margarine**
**2 tablespoons all-purpose
    flour**
½ teaspoon chervil
½ teaspoon parsley flakes
¼ teaspoon tarragon leaves
Dash white pepper

Combine rice, chicken, grapes, and celery in 2-quart microproof casserole; mix lightly. Pour milk and wine into 2-cup glass measure. Cook on HI 2 minutes; set aside. Place butter in 2-cup glass measure. Cook on HI 1 minute. Stir in flour. Cook on HI 1 minute. Briskly stir in warmed milk and wine. Stir in remaining ingredients. Pour over chicken and rice mixture. Cover with casserole lid. Cook on HI 7 to 10 minutes, or until thickened and heated through, stirring once halfway through cooking time. Let stand 2 minutes before serving.

Halved Cornish Hens ———————— 4 servings

Total Cooking Time: 15 to 16 minutes

**2 Cornish hens (1 pound
    6 ounces each), halved
    lengthwise**
**5 tablespoons dry vermouth,
    divided**
**1 envelope seasoned
    coating mix for
    chicken**
1 teaspoon thyme
**4 canned peach halves,
    drained**

Rinse Cornish hen halves; pat dry with paper towels. Brush on all sides with ¼ cup of the vermouth. Blend coating mix with thyme in a plastic bag. Shake 1 hen half at a time in plastic bag until thoroughly coated.

Arrange halves, skin-side up, with thickest portion toward outside of a 10-inch microproof pie plate. Cover with waxed paper. Cook on HI 13 to 14 minutes, or until tender.

Place peach halves, cut side-up, in center of pie plate. Divide remaining vermouth among centers of peaches. Cover with waxed paper. Cook on HI 2 minutes, or until peaches are warm.

Cracker or cornflake crumbs can be used in place of seasoned coating mix.

Swiss Chicken and Ham Roll-Ups _____ 6 servings

Total Cooking Time: 8 to 10 minutes

1½ **cups coarsely ground
     cooked chicken**
1   **can (10¾ ounces)
     condensed cream of
     chicken soup, divided**
1   **green onion, thinly sliced**
6   **slices boiled ham**
2   **cups cooked rice**
¼   **cup dairy sour cream or
     yogurt**
¼   **cup milk**
½   **cup shredded Swiss
     cheese**
     Paprika

Combine chicken, ⅓ cup soup, and onion in mixing bowl. Spoon ¼ cup chicken mixture on each ham slice and roll up. Secure with wooden toothpick, if necessary. Spread rice in shallow 1½-quart microproof dish. Place roll-ups on top of rice. Mix remaining soup with sour cream and milk. Pour over ham rolls. Cook on HI 8 to 10 minutes, rotating dish halfway through cooking time. Sprinkle with cheese and paprika. Cover and let stand 5 minutes before serving.

Mandarin Chicken and Rice _____ 4 servings

Total Cooking Time: 18 to 19 minutes

1   **can (16 ounces) chop suey
     vegetables, drained**
1   **can (10¾ ounces)
     condensed cream of
     mushroom soup**
¾   **cup quick-cooking rice**
1   **can (5.3 ounces)
     evaporated milk**
1   **can (4 ounces) mushroom
     pieces, undrained**
¼   **cup minced onion**
2   **whole chicken breasts,
     boned and halved**
     Paprika

Blend vegetables, soup, rice, milk, mushrooms with liquid, and onion in 3-quart microproof casserole. Cover. Cook on HI 5 minutes, stirring halfway through cooking time. Arrange chicken breasts on top of casserole, placing thickest parts toward outside of casserole. Cover. Cook on HI 13 to 14 minutes, or until tender. Sprinkle with paprika. Let stand, covered, 5 minutes before serving.

Chicken Steaks ——————————— makes 4 patties

Total Cooking Time: 10 to 12 minutes

1½ **cups fresh bread crumbs, divided**
1 **cup chopped cooked chicken**
⅓ **cup milk**
2 **tablespoons chopped onion**
1 **tablespoon minced fresh parsley**
¼ **teaspoon salt**
⅛ **teaspoon pepper**
½ **teaspoon paprika**
  Basic White Sauce (page 77)

Combine 1 cup bread crumbs, chicken, milk, onion, parsley, salt, and pepper in a 1½-quart bowl. Form into 4 patties. Mix paprika with remaining bread crumbs. Coat patties with crumb mixture. Place in 9-inch square microproof dish or 10-inch round microproof plate. Cook on HI 3 minutes; turn patties over. Cook on HI 3 to 4 minutes. Serve with Basic White Sauce.

Chicken Breasts with Cashews ———— 4 servings

Total Cooking Time: 25 to 30 minutes

1 **package (6 ounces) frozen pea pods**
2 **tablespoons dry white wine or water**
1 **tablespoon soy sauce**
1 **tablespoon oil**
1 **tablespoon cornstarch**
⅛ **teaspoon freshly ground pepper**
⅛ **teaspoon hot pepper sauce**
2 **whole boneless chicken breasts, skinned and flattened to ⅓-inch thickness**
1 **medium onion, sliced into rings**
1 **red or green pepper, sliced into strips**
2 **tablespoons vegetable oil**
1 **cup whole cashews, unsalted**
½ **cup chicken stock or bouillon**

Defrost pea pods on 30 for 5 minutes. Set aside. Combine wine, soy sauce, oil, cornstarch, pepper, and pepper sauce in a small bowl. Cut each whole chicken breast into 4 to 6 pieces. Add each piece to wine marinade, then place chicken in 9- or 10-inch glass pie plate. Pour remaining marinade over pieces; allow to marinate 15 to 20 minutes. Combine onion, pepper slices, and oil in a 2-quart glass bowl. Cook on HI 5 minutes, stirring once. Add cashews and chicken stock. Pour marinade into onion-oil mixture. Stir to blend well; set aside. Cook chicken pieces on HI 4 to 6 minutes. Turn pieces over. Cook on HI 4 to 5 minutes, or until chicken loses its pink color. Cover and set aside. Cover and cook sauce mixture on HI 5 to 6 minutes, or until thickened. Stir in pea pods. Spoon sauce over chicken. Cook on 80 for 2 to 3 minutes, or until heated through.

Wagonwheel Drumsticks Dinner _____ 2 servings

Total Cooking Time: 18 to 20 minutes

**4 chicken legs (about
      1 pound)**
**2 tablespoons Italian salad
      dressing**
**¼ cup Italian seasoned
      bread crumbs**
**2 potatoes (8 ounces each),
      cut in half lengthwise**
**2 tablespoons butter,
      melted**
**¼ cup Parmesan cheese
      Paprika**

Coat chicken legs with Italian dressing and bread crumbs. Arrange spoke fashion in a 10-inch round microproof dinner plate with meaty portion of leg on the outer edges. Place a potato half between each leg, skin-side down. Brush with butter and Parmesan cheese. Sprinkle with paprika. Cover with paper towel. Cook on HI 9 to 10 minutes, rotating dish once. Turn legs over and turn potatoes around. Cook on HI 9 to 10 minutes, or until legs are done, turning dish once.

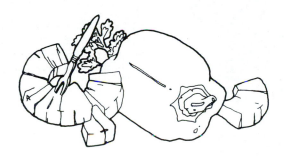

Hawaiian Chicken _____ 2 to 4 servings

Total Cooking Time: 20 to 22 minutes

**2 whole chicken breasts,
      skinned and boned**
**1 can (8 ounces) crushed
      pineapple**
**1 can (8 ounces) sliced
      water chestnuts**
¼ cup soy sauce
¼ cup chopped green pepper
2 tablespoons cornstarch
1 tablespoon onion flakes
½ teaspoon dry mustard
¼ teaspoon ginger
¼ teaspoon bead molasses

Arrange chicken breasts in 1½-quart microproof casserole. Combine remaining ingredients; blend well; pour over chicken. Cover with plastic wrap. Cook on HI 10 minutes. Rearrange chicken. Cover. Cook on HI 10 to 12 minutes, or until chicken is tender. Let stand 5 minutes before serving.

Stuffed Whole Chicken ————————— 4 servings

Total Cooking Time: 46 to 53 minutes

1 **5- to 6-pound roasting chicken**
1 **teaspoon salt**
  Bread Stuffing (below)
1 **clove garlic, halved**
1 **tablespoon browning sauce**

Remove giblets and neck from cavity. Rinse chicken and pat dry with paper towels. Rub inside with salt. Fill with stuffing; close opening with toothpicks or wood skewers. Rub skin with cut sides of garlic. Secure legs and wings to bird with string. Place, breast-side down, in microproof baking dish. Cook on HI 20 minutes. Turn chicken breast-side up. Mix 2 tablespoons drippings with browning sauce; brush mixture over chicken. Cook on HI 20 to 27 minutes, or until tender. Let stand 10 minutes before serving.

For extra-crisp skin, place the cooked chicken in a conventional oven pre-heated to 450°F. Bake 5 to 10 minutes, or until desired crispness is reached.

Bread Stuffing ——————————————— 6 cups

Total Cooking Time: 6 minutes

¼ **cup butter or margarine**
⅓ **cup chopped onion**
¼ **cup chopped celery**
3 **cups dry bread cubes**
1 **cup chicken broth or water**
2 **teaspoons parsley flakes**
½ **teaspoon salt**
⅛ **teaspoon freshly ground pepper**

Combine butter, onion, and celery in 4-cup glass measure. Cook on HI 6 minutes, or until onion is transparent. Stir in remaining ingredients. Makes enough stuffing for 5- to 6-pound roasting chicken.

Herb-Seasoned Chicken —————————— 6 servings

Total Cooking Time: 17 to 21 minutes

1 **frying chicken (2 to 2½ pounds), cut up**
½ **cup Italian seasoned bread crumbs**
1½ **teaspoons seasoned salt**
1 **teaspoon paprika**
½ **teaspoon poultry seasoning**
½ **teaspoon thyme**
¼ **cup sherry**

Rinse chicken, remove skin and pat dry with paper towels. Mix bread crumbs and seasonings in plastic bag. Brush chicken with sherry. Shake each chicken piece in plastic bag to coat. Arrange chicken, skin-side down, on microwave roasting rack or microproof baking dish with thicker portions toward outside of dish. Cover with waxed paper. Cook on HI 10 minutes. Turn chicken. Cover. Cook on HI 7 to 11 minutes, or until tender. Let stand 5 minutes before serving.

Turkey Crunch —————————— 6 servings

Total Cooking Time: 12½ to 13½ minutes

1 **tablespoon butter or margarine**
¼ **cup sliced celery**
¼ **cup chopped onion**
¼ **cup chopped green pepper**
1 **can (10¾ ounces) condensed cream of mushroom soup**
¼ **cup milk**
1 **can (5 ounces) chow mein noodles, divided**
1½ **cups diced cooked turkey or chicken**
1 **can (4 ounces) mushroom pieces, drained**
2 **tablespoons sliced pimiento**
¼ **teaspoon poultry seasoning**
¼ **teaspoon salt**

Combine butter, celery, onion, and green pepper in 2-quart microproof casserole. Cook on HI 5 minutes, or until vegetables are tender, stirring once during cooking time. Combine soup and milk in small bowl; stir into onion mixture. Stir in 2 cups chow mein noodles, turkey, mushrooms, pimiento, poultry seasoning, and salt. Cook on HI 7 to 8 minutes. Stir. Sprinkle remaining noodles around edges of casserole. Cook on HI 30 seconds. Let stand 2 minutes before serving.

Glazed Turkey Legs ——————————— 2 to 4 servings

Total Cooking Time: 28 to 29½ minutes

2 **turkey legs (2½ to 3 pounds)**
⅓ **cup honey**
1 **teaspoon grated lemon peel**
1 **teaspoon lemon juice**
1 **teaspoon cornstarch**
¼ **teaspoon bottled brown sauce**

Place turkey legs in 10-inch round or 9-inch square microproof dish; cover with paper towel. Cook on HI 11 to 12 minutes, turning once. Turn legs over. Cook on HI 12 minutes. Combine honey, lemon peel, lemon juice, cornstarch and brown sauce in a small glass bowl. Cook on HI 1 to 1½ minutes, or until thick. Brush turkey legs with half of the glaze. Cook on HI 2 minutes. Turn legs over; brush with remaining glaze. Cook on HI 2 minutes.

Orange-Glazed Duckling ——————— 4 servings

Total Cooking Time: 44 to 46 minutes

1 **duckling (3 to 4 pounds), quartered**
  Salt
  Freshly ground pepper
¾ **cup fresh orange juice**
2 **tablespoons sugar**
2 **teaspoons cornstarch**
1 **tablespoon grated fresh orange peel**
½ **teaspoon garlic powder**
1 **small orange, sectioned and each section quartered**
2 **tablespoons dry sherry**

Sprinkle both sides of duckling with salt and pepper. Pierce skin in several places with fork. Place, skin-side up, in 12 × 7-inch microproof baking dish with thickest portions toward outside of dish. Cover with waxed paper. Cook on 60 for 18 to 20 minutes, covering wings with 1-inch strip of aluminum foil halfway through cooking time. Drain; rearrange pieces, skin-side down. Cover. Cook on 60 for 8 minutes. Turn pieces skin-side up. Cover. Cook on 30 for 15 minutes, or until tender.

Combine juice, sugar, cornstarch, orange peel, and garlic powder in 2-cup glass measure. Cook on HI 3 minutes, or until thickened, stirring every 1 minute. Stir in orange sections and sherry. Arrange duck on serving platter. Pour half of sauce over duck. Pass remaining sauce.

SEAFOOD SAMPLER

Fish fillets cook best when rolled and arranged around the outside of the dish (left). Oysters and other shellfish are arranged in a circle, with the thickest parts toward the outside of the dish (above).

In microwave cooking, there's fast and then there's *fast* — seafood cooking. If you have been impressed with the cooking speed of your oven for chicken and other food, you'll be amazed at its performance with fish. For best results, have everything ready and then cook your fish last. Even standing time is short.

Seafood from the microwave oven is a quality success, too. It is so moist, tender, and delicious that you'll never want to cook it any other way. The results are excellent.

Keep in mind that fish is versatile. Most recipes that specify a particular variety will work with many substitutes. When a recipe calls for fish fillets, you can use sole, flounder, bluefish, cod, scrod, perch, or any similar fish. Fish is done when the flesh becomes opaque and barely flakes with a fork.

Converting Your Recipes

As in conventional cooking, the secret to seafood in the microwave oven is to watch it carefully, since fish can overcook in seconds. Other than that, all you need is to refer to a recipe here similar to yours, or find clues in the Guides and these tips:

- ☐ Cook fish covered unless it is coated with crumbs, which seal in the juices.
- ☐ When cooking whole fish, you should rotate the dish one-quarter turn twice during the cooking process to help provide even cooking. The odd shape of the fish requires this procedure.
- ☐ Shellfish is done when flesh is opaque and just firm
- ☐ Shellfish come in their own cooking containers, which respond well to microwave cooking. Clam and mussel shells open before your eyes. Shrimp, crab, and lobster shells turn pink.
- ☐ All seafood recipes freeze well, except where otherwise noted.
- ☐ You can use the browning dish for fillets or fish patties. Preheat, add butter or oil, and brown on one side for best results.
- ☐ To remove seafood odors from the oven, combine 1 cup water with lemon juice and cloves in a small microproof bowl. Cook on HI 4 to 5 minutes.

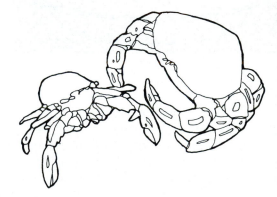

Using the Defrosting Guide

1. Remove fish and shellfish from original wrappers, and place in microproof dish. Discard any aluminum foil, metal rings, or wire twist ties.
2. To prevent the outer edges from drying out or beginning to cook, it is best to remove fish from oven before it has completely thawed.
3. Finish defrosting under cold running water, separating fillets.
4. Follow thawing with 5 minutes of standing time.

DEFROSTING GUIDE — FISH AND SHELLFISH

Food	Amount	Power Control Setting	Time (minutes)	Standing Time (minutes)	Special Notes
Fish Fillets	1 lb. 2 lbs.	30 30	4 - 6 5 - 7	5 5	Turn over. Carefully separate fillets under cold water.
Fish steaks	1 lb.	30	4 - 6	5	Carefully separate steaks under cold running water.
Whole fish	8 - 10 oz. 1½ - 2 lbs.	30 30	4 - 6 5 - 7	5 5	Shallow microproof dish; shape of fish determines size. Cover head with aluminum foil. Turn over.
Lobster tails	8 oz. package	30	5 - 7	5	Remove from package to microproof baking dish.
Crab legs	8 - 10 oz.	30	5 - 7	5	Microproof baking dish. Break apart and turn over.
Crabmeat	6 oz.	30	4 - 5	5	Defrost in package on microproof dish. Break apart. turn over.
Shrimp	1 lb.	30	3 - 4	5	Remove from package to microproof dish. Spread loosely and rearrange during thawing as necessary.
Scallops	1 lb.	30	8 - 10	5	Defrost in package if in block; spread out on microproof baking dish if in pieces. Turn over and rearrange during thawing as necessary.
Oysters, shucked	12 oz.	30	3 - 4	5	Remove from package to microproof dish. Turn over and rearrange during thawing as necessary.

Using the Cooking Guide

1. Defrost seafood fully before cooking.
2. Rinse under cold running water.
3. Place seafood in microproof baking dish with thick edges of fillets and steaks and thick ends of shellfish toward the outer edge of the dish.
4. Cover dish with plastic wrap or waxed paper.
5. When using a microwave thermometer, insert it into the meatiest part of the fish, parallel to spine of whole fish.
6. Test often during the cooking period to avoid overcooking.
7. Method and time are the same for seafood with or without the shell.

COOKING GUIDE — FISH AND SHELLFISH

Food	Power control Setting	Time (minutes)	Standing Time (minutes)	Special Notes
Fish fillets, 1 lb. ½ inch thick 2 lbs.	HI	4 - 5 7 - 8	4 - 5 4 - 5	Shallow microproof dish, covered.
Fish steaks, 1 inch thick, 1 lb.	HI	5 - 6	5 - 6	Shallow microproof dish, covered.
Whole fish 8 - 10 oz. 1½ - 2 lbs.	HI HI	3½ - 4 5 - 7	3 - 4 5	Shallow microproof dish.
Crab legs 8 - 10 oz. 16 - 20 oz.	HI HI	3 - 4 5 - 6	5 5	Shallow microproof dish, covered. Turn once.
Shrimp, scallops 8 oz. 1 lb.	70 70	3 - 4 5 - 7		Shallow microproof dish, covered. Rearrange halfway.
Snails, clams oysters, shucked 12 oz.	70	3 - 4		Shallow microproof dish, covered. Rearrange halfway.
Lobster tails 1: 8 oz. 2: 8 oz. each 4: 8 oz. each	HI HI HI	3 - 4 5 - 6 9 - 11	5 5 5	Shallow microproof dish. Split shell to reduce curling.

REHEATING GUIDE — CONVENIENCE SEAFOOD

Food	Amount	Power Control Setting	Time (minutes)	Special Notes
Shrimp croquettes	12 oz. package	80	6 - 8	Slit pouch, place on microproof plate with croquettes. Cover, turn halfway through cooking time.
Fish sticks, frozen				Follow package directions. Will not crisp. Cook on microproof serving plate
Tuna casserole, frozen	16 oz. package	HI	4 - 6	Remove from package to 1-quart casserole. Stir once during cooking and before serving.
Shrimp or crab newburg, frozen pouch	6½ oz.	HI	4 - 6	Slit pouch. Place on microproof plate. Flex pouch to mix halfway through cooking time. Stir before serving.

Fish Fillets Amandine ——————— 4 servings

Total Cooking Time: 12 to 14 minutes

⅓ **cup sliced or slivered almonds**
¼ **cup butter or margarine**
1 **pound fish fillets, cut in serving pieces**
½ **teaspoon salt**
½ **teaspoon lemon pepper**

Place almonds and butter in 1½-quart microproof baking dish. Cook on HI 6 minutes, or until almonds are golden, stirring once during cooking time. Remove almonds with slotted spoon; set aside. Add fish fillets; turn to coat both sides. Cover with plastic wrap. Cook on HI 6 to 8 minutes, or until fish flakes easily and is opaque. Sprinkle with salt, lemon pepper, and almonds. Cover and let stand 2 minutes before serving.

Poached Fish ——————— 4 servings

Total Cooking Time: 19 to 21 minutes

4 **cups water**
1 **cup white wine**
1 **stalk celery with leaves, cut up**
1 **small onion, sliced**
4 **lemon slices**
1½ **teaspoons salt**
5 **peppercorns**
1 **tablespoon minced fresh parsley**
4 **fish steaks (¾- to 1-inch thick), such as halibut or salmon**

Combine all ingredients, except fish, in 2-quart microproof casserole. Cover. Cook on HI 15 to 17 minutes, or until boiling. Strain liquid; return to casserole. Add fish; spoon liquid over top. Cover. Cook on HI 4 minutes (3 to 4 minutes per pound), or until fish flakes easily and is opaque. (To keep fish from becoming tough, do not overcook.) Let stand 3 minutes in liquid. Remove from liquid and place on serving platter.

Other liquids can be used for poaching, such as clam juice, chicken broth, or tomato juice.

Herb-Crumbed Fish Fillets _____ 4 servings

Total Cooking Time: 4 to 5 minutes

4   fish fillets (½ pound)
⅓   cup seasoned Italian
      bread crumbs
¼   cup grated Parmesan
      cheese
¼   teaspoon garlic powder
¼   teaspoon salt
1   egg white, lightly
      beaten

Rinse fillets; pat dry with paper towels; set aside. Combine crumbs, cheese, garlic powder, and salt in small bowl. Dip fillets in egg white, then in crumb mixture; coat well. Arrange fillets in shallow microproof baking dish, placing thickest part of fillets toward outside of dish. Cover with paper towel. Cook on HI 4 to 5 minutes, or until fish flakes easily. Let stand 2 minutes. Serve with lemon wedges.

Halibut and Vegetables _____ 2 servings

Total Cooking Time: 14 to 16 minutes

2   halibut steaks (6 to 8
      ounces each) or
      similar fish
2   medium carrots, split
      lengthwise and cut
      in 2-inch strips
1   small onion, chopped
1   medium potato, peeled
      and cut in thin
      2-inch strips
1   stalk celery, cut in
      thin 2-inch strips
½   green pepper, cut in
      thin 2-inch strips
1   small zucchini, cut in
      thin 2-inch strips
2   tablespoons butter or
      margarine
1   tablespoon minced fresh
      parsley
      Salt
      Freshly ground pepper
      Paprika

Rinse fish steaks; pat dry with paper towels; set aside. Combine vegetables in shallow 1-quart microproof bowl. Dot with butter. Sprinkle with salt and pepper. Cover with plastic wrap. Cook on HI 7 to 8 minutes, or until vegetables are almost tender; stir. Sprinkle with parsley. Arrange fish over vegetables, covering vegetables completely. Season lightly with salt, pepper, and paprika. Cover with plastic wrap. Cook on HI 7 to 8 minutes, or until fish flakes easily and is opaque. Let stand, covered, 3 minutes before serving.

Tuna and Vegetable Pie ——————— 6 to 8 servings

Total Cooking Time: 24 to 27 minutes

1 **can (16 ounces) stewed tomatoes, drained**
1 **cup frozen mixed vegetables, thawed**
2 **tablespoons minced onion**
2 **tablespoons all-purpose flour**
1 **teaspoon salt**
⅛ **teaspoon freshly ground pepper**
1 **can (9¼ ounces) tuna, drained and flaked**
4 **eggs, lightly beaten**
1 **cup shredded Swiss cheese**
1 **baked 9-inch Homemade Pie Shell (page 156)**
¼ **cup grated Parmesan cheese**

Combine tomatoes, mixed vegetables, and onion in 2-quart glass measure. Cook on HI 5 minutes. Add flour, salt, pepper, and tuna; blend well. Cook on HI 3 minutes, or until thickened.

Stir about ½ cup of the hot tuna mixture into eggs in small bowl; return to tuna mixture. Stir in Swiss cheese. Pour into prepared pie shell. Cook on 60 for 11 to 13 minutes, or until set in center, rotating pie at 5-minute intervals. Sprinkle top with Parmesan cheese. Let stand on heat-resistant surface, covered with foil, for 10 minutes before serving.

Tuna-Mushroom Patties ——————— 6 servings

Total Cooking Time: 9½ minutes

2 **cans (6½ ounces each) tuna, drained**
1 **can (10¾ ounces) condensed cream of celery soup, divided**
½ **cup fresh bread crumbs**
½ **cup chopped fresh mushrooms**
1 **egg, beaten**
2 **tablespoons instant minced onion**
¼ **teaspoon white pepper**
2 **tablespoons milk**
2 **tablespoons minced fresh parsley**

Combine tuna, half the can of soup, bread crumbs, mushrooms, egg, onion, and pepper in mixing bowl. Form into 6 patties (about ½ cup each). Place in shallow microproof baking dish. Cover with waxed paper. Cook on HI 8 minutes, rotating dish once during cooking time. Combine remaining soup with milk in 2-cup glass measure. Cook on HI 1½ minutes, or until heated through, stirring once during cooking time. Pour sauce over patties. Sprinkle with parsley and serve.

Cream of mushroom soup can be substituted for cream of celery soup.

Stuffed Fillet of Sole with Shrimp Sauce

————————————— 4 to 6 servings

Total Cooking Time: 11½ to 13 minutes

¼　**cup thinly sliced green onion**
¼　**cup thinly sliced celery**
1　**tablespoon finely chopped shallot**
2　**tablespoons butter or margarine**
2　**tablespoons chopped fresh parsley**
1½　**cups fresh bread crumbs**
¼　**cup tarragon**
¼　**teaspoon salt**
⅛　**teaspoon white pepper**
1½　**pounds fresh or thawed frozen sole fillets**
½　**cup dry white wine**

Sauce

3　**tablespoons butter or margarine**
2　**tablespoons all-purpose flour**
¼　**teaspoon salt**
⅛　**teaspoon white pepper**
1　**cup half-and-half or milk**
1　**egg yolk, lightly beaten**
1　**cup cooked shrimp**

Combine green onion, celery, shallot, and butter in 2-quart glass measure. Cook on 90 for 3 minutes. Blend in parsley, bread crumbs, tarragon, salt, and pepper. Divide and spoon stuffing onto fillets. Roll up; secure with toothpicks. Place fillets, seam-side down, in a 1½-quart microproof baking dish. Pour wine over fillets. Cook on HI 5 to 6 minutes, turning dish halfway through cooking time. Strain liquid through cheesecloth; reserve liquid for use in sauce.

To prepare sauce, place butter in 1-quart glass measure. Cook on HI 30 seconds. Stir in flour, salt, pepper, and half-and-half. Cook on HI 1½ minutes; stir. Spoon small amount of hot mixture into egg yolk in small bowl. Stir yolk mixture into remaining sauce. Add shrimp and reserved cooking liquid. Cook on HI 1½ to 2 minutes; stir. If thicker sauce is desired, cook on 50 for 1 minute. Spoon sauce over fillets and serve.

Stuffed Fillet of Sole with Shrimp Sauce　➡

Salmon Steak with Cucumber Sauce ———— 2 servings

Total Cooking Time: 7½ to 8½ minutes

¼ **cup finely chopped,
    peeled and seeded
    cucumber**
2 **tablespoons mayonnaise**
2 **tablespoons dairy sour
    cream**
½ **teaspoon chopped chives
    or ¼ teaspoon
    freeze-dried chives**
½ **teaspoon instant minced
    onion**
⅛ **teaspoon salt**
2 **salmon steaks (1-inch
    thick)**
   Lemon pepper

Combine cucumber, mayonnaise, sour cream, chives, onion, and salt in small bowl; set aside. Place salmon in 2 microproof au gratin dishes or one 8-inch microproof pie plate. Sprinkle with lemon pepper. Cover with plastic wrap. Cook on HI 4½ to 5½ minutes, rotating dish halfway through cooking time, or until fish flakes easily and is opaque. Drain, if necessary. Spoon cucumber sauce over salmon. Cook on 20 for 3 minutes, or until sauce is warm. Let stand 2 minutes before serving.

To prepare 4 salmon steaks, prepare cucumber sauce, doubling ingredients. Arrange salmon steaks in 10-inch round microproof dish with narrow ends in center. Cook on HI 6 to 8 minutes. Spoon Cucumber Sauce over salmon. Cook on 20 for 5 to 6 minutes, or until sauce is warm.

To reduce calories, omit the sauce and serve with lemon wedges and minced fresh parsley.

Baked Salmon Steaks ———— 2 servings

Total Cooking Time: 5 to 6 minutes

2 **salmon steaks (6 to 8
    ounces each)**
2 **teaspoons butter or
    margarine**
2 **green onions, thickly
    sliced**
2 **tablespoons fresh lemon
    juice**
½ **teaspoon salt**
¼ **teaspoon lemon pepper**

Arrange salmon in 9-inch microproof pie plate. Dot with butter; sprinkle with remaining ingredients. Cover with plastic wrap. Cook on HI 3 minutes. Turn salmon over. Cover. Cook on HI 2 to 3 minutes, or until salmon flakes easily. Let stand, covered, 2 minutes before serving. Turn onto serving platter; spoon onions and juice on top and serve.

Hawaiian Baked Fish _____ 4 to 6 servings

Total Cooking Time: 7 to 9 minutes

1 **cup pineapple juice**
2 **tablespoons butter or margarine**
1 **tablespoon minced pimiento**
1 **tablespoon instant minced onion**
1½ **teaspoons cornstarch**
1 **teaspoon parsley flakes**
½ **teaspoon tumeric**
2 **cups cooked rice**
1 **pound fresh or thawed frozen fish fillets**

Combine pineapple juice, butter, pimiento, onion, cornstarch, parsley, and tumeric in 2-cup glass measure; blend well. Cook on HI 3 to 4 minutes, or until mixture begins to thicken, stirring twice during cooking.

Spread rice in shallow 1½-quart microproof casserole. Roll up fillets and place on top of rice. Pour sauce over all. Cover with plastic wrap. Cook on HI 4 to 5 minutes, or until fish flakes easily and is opaque. Let stand, covered, 3 minutes, before serving. Garnish with pineapple, if desired.

Stuffed Bass _____ 4 servings

Total Cooking Time: 14 minutes

1 **whole bass (2 pounds), cleaned**
¼ **cup chopped onion**
2 **tablespoons butter or margarine**
¾ **cup dry bread crumbs**
½ **cup chopped mushrooms**
2 **tablespoons minced fresh parsley**
1 **large egg, beaten**
1 **tablespoon lemon juice**
½ **teaspoon salt**
⅛ **teaspoon freshly ground pepper**
1 **tablespoon bottled brown sauce**
1 **tablespoon water**

Rinse bass well in cool water and pat dry; set aside. Place onion and butter in 1½-quart microproof bowl. Place in oven. Cook on HI 2 minutes. Stir in remaining ingredients except brown sauce and water. Spoon stuffing into cavity of bass. Place on oval microproof platter or in 12 × 7-inch microproof baking dish. Combine brown sauce and water; brush over fish. Cover dish lightly with plastic wrap. Cook on HI 12 minutes. Let stand 5 minutes before serving.

Other whole fish can be substituted for bass, such as red snapper, lake trout, salmon, or whitefish.

Crab Imperial _____ 4 to 6 servings

Total Cooking Time: 14 to 15 minutes

½ **cup chopped onion**
2 **tablespoons butter or margarine**
1 **cup sliced mushrooms**
3 **tablespoons flour**
1½ **cups light cream**
3 **tablespoons dry white wine**
¼ **teaspoon salt**
⅛ **teaspoon freshly ground pepper**
2 **egg yolks, lightly beaten**
1½ **cups crab meat chunks**

Combine onion and butter in 2-quart glass measure. Cook on HI 3 minutes. Stir in mushrooms. Cook on HI 2 minutes. Add flour; blend well. Stir in cream, wine, salt, and pepper. Cook on HI 5 to 6 minutes, or until thickened. Blend in egg yolks. Cook on HI 2 minutes, stirring after 1 minute. Fold in the crab. Cook on HI 2 minutes, stirring every 30 seconds. Serve in au gratin dishes, individual custard cups, ramekins or a shell.

For an extra touch, blend 1 cup fresh bread crumbs with 2 tablespoons melted butter, and ½ teaspoon paprika. Sprinkle on each serving. Cook on 30 until hot and bubbly around edges.

Clams Casino _____ 2 servings

Total Cooking Time: 10 to 18 minutes

12 **clams**
½ **cup butter or margarine, softened**
¼ **cup finely chopped onions**
¼ **cup finely chopped green pepper**
¼ **cup finely chopped celery**
¼ **cup chopped fresh parsley**
2 **tablespoons lemon juice**
1 **jar (5 ounces) pimientos, chopped**
4 **slices bacon, cooked and crumbled**

Arrange half of clams in circle on microproof plate or serving platter, with hinges toward rim. Cook on HI 3 to 6 minutes, or until shells open; remove clams as shells open. Repeat with remaining clams. Cream butter, onions, green pepper, celery, parsley, and lemon juice in a 1-quart glass measure. Arrange half of clams in circle on microproof platter. Top each clam with equal portion of vegetable mixture, chopped pimiento, and crumbled bacon. Cook on HI 2 to 3 minutes. Repeat with remaining clams. Serve hot.

← *Crab Imperial, Clams Casino*

Scampi
2 servings

Total Cooking Time: 4½ to 6½ minutes

3 tablespoons vegetable oil
2 large cloves garlic, minced
3 tablespoons minced fresh parsley
2 tablespoons dry white wine
⅛ teaspoon paprika
¾ pound large shrimp, shelled, deveined, and butterflied, tails intact
Juice of ½ medium lemon
Salt
Freshly ground pepper
Chopped fresh parsley

Combine oil and garlic in oval microproof baking dish just large enough to hold all ingredients. Cook on HI 1 minute. Stir in minced parsley, wine, and paprika. Cook on HI 1 minute. Add shrimp. Sprinkle with lemon juice, salt, and pepper, and stir to coat well. Arrange shrimp with tails toward center of dish. Cover with waxed paper. Cook on HI 1½ to 2½ minutes. Stir; cover. Cook on HI 1 to 2 minutes. Garnish with parsley and serve.

Clams with Creamy Garlic Sauce
4 servings

Total Cooking Time: 8 to 10 minutes

24 clams in the shell, well scrubbed

Sauce
2 tablespoons finely minced onion
1 clove garlic, finely minced
2 tablespoons dry white wine
¼ teaspoon salt
⅛ teaspoon freshly ground pepper
½ cup (8 tablespoons) butter, chilled and cut into 8 pieces

Arrange half the clams in a circle on a microproof plate with hinges toward rim. Cook on HI 2 to 3 minutes, or until shells open. Remove as soon as they open. Repeat with remaining shells. Break off top shells and arrange in a circle on plate. Cover with plastic wrap. Set aside.

Combine onion, garlic, wine, salt, and pepper in a 4-cup glass measure. Cook on HI 2 minutes. Quickly whisk in 2 tablespoons butter, 1 tablespoon at a time. Return to oven. Cook on HI 30 seconds. Continue to whisk in butter, 1 tablespoon at a time, returning sauce to oven and cooking on HI for 30 seconds after each 2 tablespoons butter are added. The sauce should be creamy and slightly thickened. Spoon butter sauce on each clam. Serve hot.

HOME BAKED GOODNESS

Cakes cooked in the microwave oven are checked for doneness with the classic toothpick test (right). Typical microwave muffin ring provides even cooking (above).

Treat your family and friends to the rich aroma of a hot-from-the-oven homemade bread. For a quick and easy surprise breakfast, or as a coffee-klatch companion, you can count on fresh baked goods from the microwave oven.

Bread cooked in the microwave has excellent texture and flavor, but does not brown or develop crust. There is no hot air to dry the surface as in conventional baking. For this reason, most microwave recipes call for dark flours, or the addition of molasses and spices. The absence of a crust is beneficial, however, as it allows cakes and bread to rise much higher. For this reason, larger loaf pans are often recommended. It's also advisable to use ring molds or microproof bundt pans for more even cooking.

Are there any chocolate-covered-cherries fans at your house? If so, you'll want to start off with Chocolate Cherry Bundt Cake (page 150). Pecan Rum Pie (page 149), too, is a can't wait-to-try treat.

Converting Your Recipes

When adapting "quick bread" recipes, you will find it necessary to reduce the amount of leavening (baking powder or soda) by about one-quarter the normal amount. A bitter aftertaste is apparent if too much leavening is used in biscuits or muffins. Since food rises higher in the microwave oven, you will not see a loss in volume from the reductions of soda or baking powder. If a recipe contains buttermilk or sour cream, do not change the amount of soda, since it serves to counteract the sour taste and does not act only as a leavening agent. When using a mix where leavening cannot be reduced, allow the dough to stand about 10 minutes before cooking in order for some of the gas to be lost. And observe the following tips:

☐ Fill paper-lined muffin cups only half full to allow muffins to rise.

☐ You can prepare your own "brown 'n serve" breads and rolls by baking them ahead in the microwave oven. Then place them in the conventional oven to brown just before serving.

☐ Breads and rolls should be reheated until they are warm to the touch. Overheating or overcooking makes bread tough and rubbery.

☐ Heat bread slices on paper napkins or paper towels to absorb excess moisture.

☐ To raise yeast dough, place 1 cup water in 2-cup glass measure. Cook on HI 3 minutes, or until boiling. Place dough in oven beside water. Cook on 1 (lowest possible setting) 10 minutes. Leave dough and water in oven 20 minutes, or until dough doubles.

COOKING GUIDE — PUDDING AND PIE FILLING MIX

Food	Amount	Time (minutes)	Power Control Setting	Special Notes
Pudding and pie filling mix	3¼ ounces 5½ ounces	6½ - 7 8 - 10	HI HI	Follow package directions. Stir every 3 minutes. Use 4-cup glass measure.
Egg custard	3 ounces	8 - 10	70	Follow package directions. Stir every 3 minutes. Use 4-cup glass measure.
Tapioca	3¼ ounces	6 - 7	HI	Follow package directions. Stir every 3 minutes. Use 4-cup glass measure.

COOKING/REHEATING GUIDE — CONVENIENCE BREADS

Food	Power Control Setting	Time	Special Notes
Hamburger buns, hot dog rolls, frozen: 1 lb.	30	1 - 2 minutes	Place on paper plate or towels.
Room temp.: 1 2 4 6	80 80 80 80	5 - 10 seconds 10 - 15 seconds 15 - 20 seconds 20 - 25 seconds	Wrap in paper towel.
Doughnuts, 1 sweet rolls, 2 muffins 4 6	80 80 80 80	10 - 15 seconds 20 - 25 seconds 35 - 40 seconds 45 - 50 seconds	Place on paper plate or towel. Add 15 seconds if frozen.
Whole coffee cake, frozen, 10 - 13 oz. Room temp.: 10 - 13 oz.	80 80	1½ - 2 minutes 1 - 1½ minutes	Place on paper plate or towel. Place on paper plate or towel.
French bread, frozen: 1 lb. Room temp.: 1 lb.	80 80	1½ - 2 minutes 20 - 30 seconds	Place on paper plate or towel
English muffins, waffles, frozen: 2	HI	30 - 45 seconds	Place on paper towels. Toast in toaster after defrosting, if desired.
Corn bread mix: 9 oz.	HI	2 - 3 minutes	Use paper-lined microproof muffin pan. Turn pan if rising unevenly. Let stand 2 minutes before serving.
Nut bread mix: 15 - 17 oz.	HI	15 minutes	Use 8-cup microproof ring mold. Let stand 5 minutes before serving.
Blueberry muffin mix: 15 oz.	HI	2 - 3 minutes	Use 6 paper-lined custard cups or microproof muffin pan. Let stand 2 minutes before serving.
Bread, frozen 1 slice 1 lb. loaf	30 30	15 - 20 seconds 2 - 3 minutes	Place on paper plate or towels. Let stand 5 minutes before serving. In original plastic bag, remove twister. Let stand 5 minutes before serving.
Coffeecake mix: 19 oz.	50 HI	10 minutes 4 - 6 minutes	Use 9" round dish. Turn dish if rising unevenly. Let stand 5 minutes before serving.

Honey Corn Bread Ring ———————— 16 servings

Total Cooking Time: 8 to 10 minutes

1 **cup all-purpose flour**
1 **cup cornmeal**
¾ **cup milk**
⅓ **cup honey**
¼ **cup vegetable shortening**
2 **eggs**
4 **teaspoons baking powder**

Combine all ingredients in mixing bowl. Beat just until blended. Pour into lightly greased 8-cup microproof ring mold. Cook on HI 8 to 10 minutes, or until toothpick inserted near center comes out clean. If ring is rising unevenly, rotate dish. Let stand 5 minutes before unmolding onto serving plate or cutting board.

Pineapple Zucchini Bread ———————— 12 to 18 servings

Total Cooking Time: 15 to 17 minutes

½ **cup vegetable oil**
¾ **cup sugar**
2 **eggs**
1 **can (8¼ ounces) crushed pineapple**
1 **cup grated zucchini (1 medium)**
1¾ **cups all-purpose flour**
½ **teaspoon baking powder**
½ **teaspoon baking soda**
1 **teaspoon cinnamon**
½ **cup chopped nuts**

Lightly grease and sugar 8-cup microproof ring mold; set aside.
  Combine oil, sugar, and eggs in mixing bowl; blend well. Add pineapple, zucchini, flour, baking powder, baking soda, and cinnamon; mix well. Stir in nuts. Pour into prepared ring mold; spread evenly. Cook on 70 for 15 to 17 minutes, or until bread tests done. Place pan on heat-resistant surface for 10 minutes. Remove from mold; cool before slicing.

Honey Corn Bread Ring, Pineapple Zucchini Bread ➡

Pumpkin Cupcakes ———————— 12 servings

Total Cooking Time: 12¼ to 14½ minutes

1   **egg**
½   **cup firmly packed
      brown sugar**
¼   **cup sugar**
6   **tablespoons vegetable oil**
½   **cup canned or mashed
      cooked pumpkin**
½   **teaspoon vanilla**
1   **cup all-purpose flour**
2   **tablespoons milk**
½   **teaspoon cinnamon**
½   **teaspoon salt**
¼   **teaspoon baking powder**
¼   **teaspoon baking soda**
⅛   **teaspoon ginger**
      **Cream Cheese Frosting
      (page 156)**

Beat egg, sugars, and oil in mixing bowl until smooth. Blend in pumpkin and vanilla. Add remaining ingredients, except frosting; stir until smooth. Line 6 cups in microproof cupcake pan or 6 glass custard cups with paper liners. Fill half full with batter. Cook on 30 for 6 to 7 minutes, or until cupcakes test done, rotating cups if rising unevenly. Repeat with remaining batter. Cool and frost with Cream Cheese Frosting.

Peanutty
Chocolate Cake ———————— 8 to 10 servings

Total Cooking Time: 15 to 17 minutes

1   **package (18 ounces)
      yellow cake mix**
½   **cup creamy peanut butter**
4   **eggs**
¾   **cup water**
⅓   **cup vegetable oil**
1   **cup chopped unsalted
      peanuts, divided**
1   **cup chocolate chips,
      divided**

Combine cake mix, peanut butter, eggs, water, and oil in a large bowl. Beat on medium speed for 3 minutes. Pour one-third of the batter into a 12-cup microproof bundt pan. Sprinkle ⅓ cup each of the peanuts and chocolate chips over the batter. Pour another one-third of the batter carefully over peanuts and chocolate chips. Sprinkle another ⅓ cup each of the peanuts and chocolate chips over the batter. Repeat with remaining batter, peanuts, and chocolate chips. Cook on 70 for 15 to 17 minutes. Let stand 10 minutes. Invert onto serving platter.

Cheesecake and Raspberry Sauce _____ 6 to 8 servings

Total Cooking Time: 13 to 16½ minutes

¾ **cup graham cracker crumbs**
¾ **cup sugar, divided**
3 **tablespoons butter or margarine**
2 **tablespoons brown sugar**
1 **teaspoon cinnamon**
1 **package (8 ounces) cream cheese, quartered**
2 **eggs**
1 **teaspoon vanilla**
1 **cup dairy sour cream Raspberry Sauce (page 169)**

Combine crumbs, 2 tablespoons of sugar, butter, brown sugar, and cinnamon in 8-inch round microproof cake dish. Cook on HI 1 minute. Stir to combine. Press crumbs evenly over bottom and sides of cake dish.

Place cream cheese in small microproof bowl. Cook on 30 for 30 seconds, or until softened. Gradually beat in ½ cup of sugar until dissolved. Add eggs and vanilla; mix well. Pour into prepared crust. Cook on HI 4 to 5 minutes, or until nearly set in center, rotating dish if cake is cooking unevenly.

Combine sour cream and remaining 2 tablespoons sugar in small bowl; blend well. Spread carefully and evenly over filling. Cook on HI 1 to 1½ minutes, rotating after 1 minute. Edges should be set and center still soft. Cool to room temperature. Refrigerate at least 12 hours. Pass Raspberry Sauce with sliced cheesecake.

Pecan Rum Pie _____ 6 to 8 servings

Total Cooking Time: 9½ to 11½ minutes

¼ **cup butter or margarine**
1½ **cups pecan halves**
1 **cup sugar**
½ **cup dark corn syrup**
3 **eggs, lightly beaten**
1 **teaspoon rum flavoring or vanilla extract**
1 **baked (9-inch) pie shell in microproof dish**

Place butter in 2-quart glass measure or microproof bowl. Cook on HI 30 seconds, or until melted. Blend in nuts, sugar, corn syrup, eggs, and rum. Pour into pie shell. Cook on HI 9 to 11 minutes, or until center is set. Cool to room temperature before serving.

Chocolate Cherry Bundt Cake ⎯⎯ 10 to 12 servings

Total Cooking Time: 32½ to 34½ minutes

1 **tablespoon sugar**
1 **package (18½ ounces)**
   chocolate cake mix
   with pudding
1 **cup cherry pie filling**
3 **eggs**
¾ **cup water**
¼ **cup vegetable oil**
1 **teaspoon almond extract**
   White Cap Glaze (below)

Generously grease 12-cup microproof bundt pan; chill. Sprinkle with 1 tablespoon sugar; shake well to coat. Mix remaining ingredients, except glaze, following cake package directions. Pour carefully into prepared pan. Cook on 30 for 32 to 34 minutes, or until cake tests done, rotating if cake is rising unevenly. Let stand 10 minutes before inverting onto serving plate to cool. Drizzle White Cap Glaze over cake. Let stand until glaze sets. Serve.

White Cap Glaze ⎯⎯⎯⎯⎯⎯⎯⎯ ½ cup

Total Cooking Time: 30 seconds

1 **package (3 ounces)**
   cream cheese
¾ **cup confectioners sugar**
3 **to 4 teaspoons milk**

Remove foil from cream cheese. Place in 1-quart microproof bowl. Cook on 30 for 30 seconds, or until softened. Beat in sugar and milk until smooth.

Sweet Cardamom Rolls ⎯⎯⎯⎯ 6 servings

Total Cooking Time: 2½ to 3 minutes

1 **tablespoon butter or**
   margarine, softened
2 **tablespoons brown sugar**
¼ **teaspoon ground**
   cardamom
1 **package (8½ ounces)**
   refrigerator butter-
   flake rolls
1 **tablespoon finely**
   chopped nuts
   Nutmeg

Cream butter, brown sugar, and cardamom in small bowl until light; set aside. Separate refrigerator rolls. Spread a little of the butter mixture between 3 or 4 layers of dough of each roll. Stand rolls in paper-lined microproof muffin pan. Sprinkle with nuts and nutmeg. Cook on HI 2½ to 3 minutes. Let stand 2 minutes before serving.

Chocolate Cherry Bundt Cake ➜

Raisin-Oatmeal Muffins ———————— 18 servings

Total Cooking Time: 6 to 12 minutes

   1   **cup all-purpose flour**
   ⅔   **cup quick-cooking
        oatmeal**
   ¼   **cup firmly packed brown
        sugar**
   1   **teaspoon baking powder**
   ½   **teaspoon baking soda**
   ½   **teaspoon salt**
1 ½   **teaspoons cinnamon,
        divided**
   2   **eggs**
   ½   **cup vegetable oil**
   ½   **cup buttermilk**
   ½   **cup raisins**
   2   **tablespoons sugar**

Combine flour, oatmeal, brown sugar, baking powder, baking soda, salt, and ½ teaspoon cinnamon in small mixing bowl. Add eggs, oil, buttermilk, and raisins. Stir until just moistened. Spoon batter into paper-lined micro-proof muffin pan, filling each compartment about half full. Mix remaining cinnamon and sugar. Sprinkle top of each muffin with about ¼ teaspoon cinnamon-sugar mixture. Cook on HI 2 to 4 minutes, rotating cups or pan if muffins are rising unevenly. Repeat with remaining batter. Serve warm.

Blueberry Muffins ———————— 18 muffins

Total Cooking Time: 6 to 7½ minutes

1 ½   **cups all-purpose flour**
   ⅓   **cup firmly packed
        brown sugar**
   1   **teaspoon cinnamon**
   ½   **teaspoon baking
        powder**
   ½   **teaspoon baking
        soda**
   ½   **teaspoon salt**
   ¾   **cup buttermilk**
   1   **egg**
   ¼   **cup vegetable oil**
   ⅔   **cup fresh or frozen
        blueberries; thaw,
        if frozen**

Combine flour, sugar, cinnamon, baking powder, baking soda, and salt in large mixing bowl. Add buttermilk, egg, and oil; mix quickly just until moistened. Stir in blueberries. Spoon batter into paper-lined microproof muffin pan, filling each compartment half full. Cook on HI 2 to 2½ minutes, or until muffins test done, rotating pan if muffins are rising unevenly. Let stand 2 minutes. Repeat with remaining batter. Serve warm.

Chopped cranberries can be substituted for blueberries.

Butter Pecan
Ice Cream Pie
6 to 8 servings

Total Cooking Time: 4 to 5 minutes

**6 tablespoons butter or
margarine**
¾ cup all-purpose flour
**¾ cup finely ground
pecans, divided**
3 tablespoons brown sugar
**1 quart butter pecan
ice cream**

Place butter in 4-cup glass measure. Cook on HI 1 minute, or until melted. Stir in flour, half of the pecans, and sugar; mix well. Press mixture firmly onto bottom and sides of 9-inch microproof pie plate. Cook on HI 3 to 4 minutes, rotating halfway through cooking time. Cool to room temperature. Spoon ice cream into shell. (If ice cream is very firm, place carton on microproof plate. Cook on 30 for 1 to 2 minutes, or until softened.) Sprinkle remaining pecans over top. Freeze until firm.

Deep-Dish Apple
and Cheese Pie
6 to 8 servings

Total Cooking Time: 10 to 12 minutes

**7 cooking apples,
peeled, cored and
sliced (6 cups)**
**½ cup plus 3 teaspoons
sugar, divided**
**2 tablespoons all-purpose
flour**
**1 teaspoon cinnamon,
divided**
¼ teaspoon nutmeg
**¾ cup shredded
Cheddar cheese**
1 cup cake flour
**1¼ teaspoons baking
powder**
¾ teaspoon salt
**2 tablespoons butter or
margarine**
⅓ cup milk

Combine apples, ½ cup sugar, flour, ½ teaspoon cinnamon, and nutmeg in large bowl; blend well. Pour into 10 × 2-inch microproof deep dish pie plate. Sprinkle with cheese; set aside. In separate bowl, combine cake flour, baking powder, salt, 1½ teaspoons of the sugar, and butter until fine crumbs form. Add milk; stir until dough forms a ball. Roll out on floured surface to 11-inch circle. Fit over apples and cheese. Pinch edges; prick top with fork. Combine remaining sugar and cinnamon. Sprinkle over top of crust. Cook on HI 10 to 12 minutes, or until apples are tender and pastry looks dry and blistered. Serve warm or cool.

Crunchy Apple Pie ———————— 6 to 8 servings

Total Cooking Time: 11 to 15 minutes

1 baked 9-inch Homemade Pie Shell (page 156)
5 cups sliced tart apples (about 6 apples)
½ cup plus 3 tablespoons sugar, divided
½ cup all-purpose flour, divided
2 teaspoons cinnamon, divided
¾ cup dairy sour cream
⅔ cup crisp rice cereal
¼ teaspoon nutmeg
¼ cup butter or margarine, softened
⅛ teaspoon grated lemon peel

Cook Homemade Pie Shell according to directions; set aside.

Combine apples, ½ cup of the sugar, 2 tablespoons of the flour, 1 teaspoon of the cinnamon, and sour cream in mixing bowl; blend well. Pour into crust. Combine remaining 6 tablespoons flour, 3 tablespoons sugar, 1 teaspoon cinnamon, cereal, nutmeg, butter, and lemon peel in small bowl; blend well. Sprinkle over apples. Cook on HI 6 to 9 minutes, or until apples are tender. Rotate dish, if apples are cooking unevenly. Cool before serving.

Molasses Buttermilk Bread ——— 10 to 12 servings

Total Cooking Time: 9 to 10 minutes

½ cup all-purpose flour
½ cup whole wheat flour
½ cup cornmeal
1 teaspoon baking soda
½ teaspoon salt
1 egg, lightly beaten
1 cup buttermilk
⅓ cup molasses
2 tablespoons vegetable oil
⅓ cup raisins or currants

Lightly grease 8-cup microproof ring mold; set aside. Combine flours, cornmeal, baking soda, and salt in mixing bowl; mix lightly. In separate bowl combine egg, buttermilk, molasses, and oil; blend well. Add liquid ingredients to dry ingredients; blend well. Stir in raisins. Pour batter into prepared ring mold. Cook on 70 for 9 to 10 minutes, or until toothpick inserted near center comes out clean, rotating dish if bread is rising unevenly. Let stand 10 minutes on heat-resistant surface before removing from pan. Cool before slicing.

Banana Cake ———————————— 10 to 12 servings

Total Cooking Time: 6¾ to 8 minutes

¼ **cup butter or margarine,**
   room temperature
½ **cup sugar**
1 **egg**
2 **medium bananas, mashed**
1 **teaspoon vanilla**
¼ **cup milk**
1½ **cups all-purpose flour**
½ **teaspoon baking soda**
½ **teaspoon salt**
½ **teaspoon lemon juice**
½ **cup chopped nuts**

Combine butter, sugar, egg, bananas, vanilla, and milk in large mixing bowl; blend well. Stir in flour, baking soda, salt, lemon juice, and nuts. Pour into 8-cup microproof ring mold. Cook on HI 6½ to 7½ minutes, or until cake tests done. Rotate dish if cake is rising unevenly. Cool on heat-resistant surface. Frost with Cream Cheese Frosting (page 156), or sprinkle with confectioners sugar, if desired.

Classic Coconut Cake ——————— 10 to 12 servings

Total Cooking Time: 17 to 20 minutes

1 **package (18½ ounces)**
   white cake mix
½ **cup shredded coconut,**
   finely chopped
1½ **teaspoons grated lemon**
   peel

Frosting

1 **cup sugar**
½ **cup water**
¼ **teaspoon cream of tartar**
   Dash of salt
2 **egg whites**
1 **teaspoon vanilla**
1 **cup shredded coconut**

Prepare cake mix according to package directions. Fold in coconut and lemon peel. Pour half of batter into 9-inch microproof cake pan. Cook on HI 5½ to 7 minutes, or until cake tests done. Let stand 5 minutes on flat, heat-resistant surface. Transfer to wire rack; let cool. Repeat with remaining batter.

To prepare frosting, combine sugar, water, cream of tartar, and salt in a 2-cup glass measure. Cook on HI 6 minutes. In a small mixing bowl, beat egg whites with an electric mixer until soft peaks form. Gradually add hot syrup mixture to egg whites, beating continuously. Continue beating 5 minutes, or until mixture is thick and fluffy. While beating, add vanilla. Frost cake and sprinkle with coconut on top and sides.

Homemade Pie Shell ———————— one 9-inch pie shell
Total Cooking Time: 5 to 6 minutes

1 **cup all-purpose flour**
1 **teaspoon salt**
6 **tablespoons shortening**
2 **tablespoons ice water**

Place flour and salt in small bowl. Use pastry blender or 2 knives to cut in shortening until mixture resembles small peas. Sprinkle water over mixture. Stir with fork until mixture holds together; gather into a ball. Roll out on floured pastry board to 12-inch circle. Ease into 9-inch glass pie plate. Trim and flute edge. Prick pastry with fork. Cook on HI 5 to 6 minutes. Pastry is done when it looks dry and blistered. Cool. Fill as desired.

Cream Cheese Frosting ———————— 1½ cups
Total Cooking Time: 15 to 30 seconds

1 **package (3 ounces) cream cheese**
2 **tablespoons butter or margarine**
2 **cups confectioners sugar**
½ **teaspoon vanilla**
1 **to 2 teaspoons milk**

Combine cream cheese and butter in 1-quart microproof bowl. Cook on HI 15 to 30 seconds, or until softened. Beat in sugar, vanilla, and enough milk for spreading consistency.

Rice Pie Crust ———————— one 9-inch pie shell
Total Cooking Time: 1 to 1½ minutes

1½ **cups cooked rice**
1 **egg, lightly beaten**
⅓ **cup shredded Cheddar cheese**
1 **tablespoon parsley flakes**

Combine all ingredients in mixing bowl; mix well. Press evenly over bottom and sides of 9-inch glass pie plate. Cook on HI 1 to 1½ minutes, or until cheese is melted.

This crust is naturally low in calories. It can be used with many different fillings and is especially nice as the base for Onion Pie in Rice Crust (page 79).

Savory Cheese Bread _____ 2 loaves

Total Cooking Time: 14 to 16 minutes

  1 **cup milk**
  ½ **cup butter or**
      margarine
2¾ **cups all-purpose flour**
  2 **tablespoons sugar**
  ½ **teaspoon salt**
  1 **package (1 ounce)**
      active dry yeast
  1 **egg**
  1 **envelope onion soup**
      mix, divided
  1 **cup shredded**
      Cheddar cheese,
      divided

Combine milk and butter in 2-cup glass measure. Cook on HI 2 minutes. Mix flour, sugar, salt, and yeast in large mixing bowl. Add milk mixture and egg. Mix 2 tablespoons of soup mix and ¼ cup of cheese in small bowl; set aside. Add remaining soup mix and cheese to batter.

Divide batter evenly between 2 well greased 8 × 4-inch microproof loaf pans. Sprinkle with reserved onion-cheese mixture. Cover lightly. Let rise in warm place, free from draft, 1 to 1½ hours, or until double in volume. Cook 1 loaf at a time. Cook on HI 6 to 7 minutes, or until bread springs back when lightly touched, sides recede from pan, and top is no longer moist. Repeat with remaining loaf. Turn out of pans and cool on wire rack.

Garlic Bread _____ 12 servings

Total Cooking Time: 1 to 2 minutes

  1 **loaf (16 ounces) French,**
      Italian, or sourdough
      bread
  ½ **cup butter or margarine,**
      softened
  2 **cloves garlic, minced or**
      1 teaspoon garlic
      powder
  ½ **cup grated Parmesan**
      or Romano cheese
      Paprika

Cut loaf in 1-inch thick slices without cutting through bottom crust. Blend butter and garlic in small bowl. Spread on bread slices; then sprinkle with cheese and paprika. Place loaf on paper towel-lined microproof plate. Cook on HI 1 to 2 minutes, or until heated through.

Onion Herb Bread ——————————— 12 servings
Total Cooking Time: 1 to 2 minutes

1 loaf (16 ounces) French, Italian, or sourdough bread
½ cup butter or margarine, softened
1 tablespoon instant onion flakes
1 tablespoons minced fresh parsley
½ teaspoon dillweed
¼ teaspoon onion salt
Paprika

Cut loaf in 1-inch thick slices without cutting through bottom crust. Blend remaining ingredients, except paprika in small bowl. Spread on bread slices. Sprinkle with paprika. Place loaf on paper towel-lined microproof plate. Cook on HI 1 to 2 minutes, or until heated through.

Brown & Serve Rolls ——————— 6 or 12 dinner rolls
Total Cooking Time: 15 to 18 minutes

1 loaf (1 pound) frozen bread dough

Place frozen dough on lightly greased 9-inch pie plate. Fill a 1-cup glass measure with water. Cook on HI 3 to 4 minutes, or until water boils. Move water to rear of oven. Cover dough with a damp cloth. Place in oven. Cook on 20 for 5 minutes; turn loaf over. Cook on 20 for 5 minutes. Dough may now be worked and shaped. Form into twelve rolls or eighteen ¾-inch balls. Place rolls in greased microproof baking dish, or three ¾-inch balls into each greased muffin cup. Set dough aside in a warm draft-free area until it doubles in size. When doubled, cook on·HI 2 to 4 minutes, rotating dish twice. When rolls are done, the center should spring back when lightly touched. Refrigerate or freeze until ready to serve. Brown in a toaster oven or conventional oven at 425°F before serving.

SPECIAL TREATS

Carefully select the microproof cookware for bar cookies (left). If you don't have a microproof candy thermometer, use a conventional thermometer, outside the oven (above).

If you're like many cooks, making candy seems just too difficult to bother with. That is about to change, and you'll never regret it! The fuss and mess of double boilers has been eliminated by the microwave oven. Without a doubt, making candy is so easy that you'll soon laugh to yourself as friends are amazed by your talent.

You'll also soon be churning out an array of bar cookies that will have a line of neighborhood kids at your kitchen door. Raisin Nut Bars (page 165) and Brownies (page 166) were the favorites of the test kitchen, but be sure to try your own recipes, too, and others here.

Fruit specialties and sauces are also excellent and easier than — well, *everything* is easy in the microwave, isn't it?

We hope you've enjoyed this book and, more importantly, are convinced that the world of microwave cooking is a special treat of its own. Good fortune and good cooking to you!

Converting Your Recipes

To make candy, simply find a similar recipe here. You'll be trying all those recipes you've been longing to do. For other desserts, consult these tips as well as similar recipes:

- ☐ You can enhance your light batter cookies and cakes with cinnamon, nutmeg, brown sugar, coffee, nuts, toppings, frostings, glazes, food coloring, etc.
- ☐ Small drop cookies and slice 'n bake cookies don't do as well as the larger bar cookies. Drop cookies must be cooked in small batches; they tend to cook unevenly, and need to be removed individually from the oven when finished.
- ☐ A serviceable cookie sheet can be made by covering cardboard with waxed paper.
- ☐ For even cooking, select fruit of uniform size to be cooked whole, as in baked apples, or to be cooked in pieces, as in apple pie.
- ☐ Stirring sauces quickly two or three times during cooking is sufficient to ensure even cooking. Too many stirrings may slow cooking.

REHEATING GUIDE - CONVENIENCE DESSERTS

Food	Amount	Power Control Setting	Time	Special Notes
Brownies, other bars, frozen	12 - 13 oz.	30	2 - 3 minutes	Place on microproof plate. Let stand 5 minutes.
Cookies, frozen	6	30	50 - 60 seconds	Place on paper plate or towels.
Cupcakes or crumb cakes, frozen	1 or 2	30	½ - 1 minute	Place on shallow microproof plate.
Cheesecake, frozen	17 - 19 oz.	30	4 - 5 minutes	Remove from foil pan to microproof plate. Let stand 1 minute.
Pound cake, frozen	10¾ oz.	30	2 minutes	Remove from foil pan to microproof plate. Rotate once. Let stand 5 minutes.
Cake, frozen 2- or 3-layer	17 oz.	30	2½ - 3 minutes	Remove from foil pan to microproof plate. Watch carefully, frosting melts fast. Let stand 5 minutes.
Custard pie, frozen	9" pie	70	4 - 5½ minutes	Remove from foil pan to microproof pie plate. Center should be nearly set.
Fruit pie, frozen, 2 - 3 lbs	9" pie			Follow package directions.
Frozen fruit	10 oz.	HI	5 - 5½ minutes	Slit pouch. Place on microproof plate. Flex halfway through cooking time to mix. Remove from bag. Place in glass casserole, cover. Stir halfway through cooking time.
	16 oz.	HI	7 - 9 minutes	
Cake mix, single layer	9 oz.	50 HI	5 - 9 minutes 1 - 2 minutes	Use 9-inch round microproof baking dish. Rotate if rising unevenly. Let stand 5 minutes; invert onto serving plate.

Chocolate Fudge —————————————— 3 pounds
Total Cooking Time: 11 to 12 minutes

3 cups sugar
½ cup butter or margarine
1 can (5⅓ ounces)
    evaporated milk
2 cups (12 ounces)
    semisweet chocolate
    pieces
1 jar (7 ounces)
    marshmallow creme
1 cup chopped nuts
1 teaspoon vanilla

Lightly butter a 13 × 9-inch baking pan. Combine sugar, butter, and milk in 2-quart glass measure. Cook on HI 11 to 12 minutes, or until a small amount dropped in cold water forms a soft ball (234°F on microproof candy thermometer). Stir in chocolate pieces and marshmallow creme until mixture is thoroughly blended. Stir in nuts and vanilla. Pour into prepared pan. Refrigerate until firm. Cut into squares.

Chocolate-Raisin Nut Clusters ————— 1½ pounds
Total Cooking Time: 2 to 4 minutes

1 pound semisweet
    chocolate
1 cup cashews
½ cup raisins

Place chocolate in 2-quart glass measure or bowl. Cook on HI 2 to 4 minutes, or until softened. (Chocolate will not appear melted until stirred.) Stir in nuts and raisins. Drop mixture by teaspoonfuls onto waxed paper. Let stand until firm. If mixture in bowl becomes firm before being spooned onto waxed paper, cook on 30 for 1 to 2 minutes.

Penuche Fudge ——————————————— 2½ dozen
Total Cooking Time: 11 to 13 minutes

2½ cups firmly packed brown
    sugar
¾ cup milk
1 tablespoon butter or
    margarine
1 teaspoon light corn syrup
⅛ teaspoon salt
½ cup chopped nuts
1 teaspoon vanilla

Butter 8-inch square pan; set aside. Combine sugar, milk, butter, syrup, and salt in 3-quart microproof casserole. Cook on HI 5 minutes, or until sugar is dissolved. Stir. Cook on HI 6 to 8 minutes, or until small drop forms soft ball in cold water or candy thermometer registers 238°F. Cool to lukewarm. Beat with electric mixer until mixture begins to thicken. Add nuts and vanilla. Beat until mixture is very thick. Pour into prepared pan; spread evenly. Cool until firm. Cut into squares.

Fairy Food ————————————————————— 1 pound
Total Cooking Time: 14 to 18 minutes

1 **cup sugar**
1 **cup dark corn syrup**
1 **tablespoon vinegar**
1 **tablespoon baking soda**
1 **pound semisweet dipping
   chocolate**
1 **tablespoon shortening**

Line 8-inch square baking dish with aluminum foil; butter generously; set aside. Combine sugar, corn syrup, and vinegar in 2-quart glass measure or microproof bowl. Cook on HI 3 minutes, stirring several times during cooking time. Continue to cook on HI 9 to 12 minutes, or until mixture is thickened and microproof candy thermometer registers 300°F (or a small amount dropped in cold water separates into hard, brittle threads). Quickly stir in baking soda; blend well. Pour into prepared dish. Spread evenly with spoon or tip baking dish to cover bottom evenly. Let stand 1 hour, or until firm. Break hardened mixture into pieces; set aside.

Break up chocolate and place in 2-quart glass measure. Add shortening. Cook on HI 2 to 3 minutes, or until melted, stirring once during cooking. Dip hardened pieces in chocolate, covering completely. Place on waxed paper to cool. Store in refrigerator in an airtight container.

Chocolate Almond Bark ———————————— 1½ pounds
Total Cooking Time: 8 to 10 minutes

1 **cup blanched whole
   almonds**
1 **teaspoon butter or
   margarine**
1 **pound semisweet or milk
   chocolate**

Combine almonds and butter in 9-inch glass pie plate. Cook on HI 5 to 6 minutes, or until almonds are golden, stirring twice during cooking time; set aside. Place chocolate in 2-quart glass measure. Cook on HI 3 to 4 minutes, or until melted. Stir in almonds. Pour onto waxed paper-lined baking sheet. Spread to desired thickness. Refrigerate until firm. Break into pieces to serve. Store in cool place.

Dry-Roasted Peanut Brittle _____ about 1 pound

Total Cooking Time: 9 to 11 minutes

1 **cup sugar**
½ **cup light corn syrup**
1 **cup raw unsalted peanuts**
1 **tablespoon butter or margarine**
1 **teaspoon vanilla**
1 **teaspoon baking soda**

Generously grease baking sheet. Combine sugar and corn syrup in 2-quart microproof bowl. Cook on HI 4 minutes. Stir in peanuts with wooden spoon. Cook on HI 5 to 7 minutes, or until mixture reaches 300°F on microproof candy thermometer (or a small amount separates into hard, brittle threads when dropped in cold water). Stir in butter and vanilla. Blend in baking soda; stir until mixture is light and foamy. Pour onto prepared sheet; spread quickly. As candy cools, stretch into thin sheet using buttered hands. Cool completely. Break into pieces and store in an airtight container.

Pantry Fruit Salad _____ 6 servings

Total Cooking Time: 10 to 11 minutes

¼ **cup firmly packed brown sugar**
2 **teaspoons curry powder**
1 **teaspoon cornstarch**
2 **tablespoons butter or margarine**
1 **can (8½ ounces) sliced peaches, drained**
1 **can (8½ ounces) sliced pears, drained**
1 **can (11 ounces) mandarin orange segments, drained**
1 **can (8 ounces) chunk pineapple, drained**
½ **cup maraschino cherries, drained**

Combine sugar, curry, and cornstarch in 2-quart glass measure. Add butter. Cook on HI 1 minute, or until butter is melted; stir. Add all fruit; stir gently. Cook on 50 for 9 to 10 minutes, or until hot, stirring carefully once during cooking time. Let stand 5 minutes before serving. Serve warm with lamb, pork, or ham.

Poached Pears _____ 8 servings

Total Cooking Time: 11 to 13 minutes

4 cups water, divided
3 tablespoons lemon juice
4 firm, ripe pears (6 to 8 ounces each)
1 cup dry red wine
⅓ cup sugar
1 cinnamon stick
Lemon peel strip

Combine 3 cups of water and lemon juice in mixing bowl. Peel pears; cut in half lengthwise; core. Place pears in lemon-water. Combine remaining water, wine, sugar, cinnamon, and lemon peel in 2-quart microproof casserole. Cook on HI 5 minutes. Remove pears from water with slotted spoon; add to hot wine mixture. Turn pear halves to coat completely. Cover with waxed paper. Cook on HI 6 to 8 minutes, or until pears are tender, turning pears twice during cooking time. Let stand, in syrup, until cool. Serve in sherbet dishes.

Pecan Dream Bars _____ 32 bars

Total Cooking Time: 11½ to 14½ minutes

⅓ cup butter or margarine
1⅓ cups firmly packed brown sugar, divided
1⅓ cups all-purpose flour
2 eggs
3 tablespoons all-purpose flour
½ teaspoon baking powder
¼ teaspoon salt
1 teaspoon vanilla
1½ cups flaked coconut
½ cup chopped pecans
Confectioners sugar

Place butter in 8-inch square microproof baking dish. Cook on HI 30 seconds, or until softened. Blend in ⅓ cup brown sugar. Blend in 1⅓ cups flour until crumbly. Press into bottom of dish. Cook on HI 3 to 4 minutes, or until puffy. Beat eggs in mixing bowl until light and foamy. Beat in 1 cup brown sugar. Stir in 3 tablespoons flour, baking powder, salt, and vanilla. Stir in coconut and pecans. Pour over crust, spreading evenly. Cook on 80 for 8 to 10 minutes, or until set, rotating dish if mixture is cooking unevenly. Cool on wire rack. Sprinkle with confectioners sugar.

Date-Orange Bars _____ 3 dozen

Total Cooking Time: 9½ to 11½ minutes

1 **cup chopped dates**
2 **tablespoons sugar**
1 **tablespoon orange juice**
1 **teaspoon all-purpose flour**
1 **teaspoon grated orange peel**
½ **cup chopped nuts**
½ **cup butter or margarine**
¾ **cup firmly packed brown sugar**
1 **cup all-purpose flour**
1 **cup quick-cooking oatmeal**
¼ **teaspoon salt**

Combine dates, sugar, juice, flour, and orange peel in 2-quart glass measure or microproof bowl. Cook on HI 2 to 3 minutes, or until mixture is boiling, stirring once. Stir in nuts; set aside. Place butter in 9-inch round microproof baking dish. Cook on HI 30 seconds. Blend in brown sugar. Stir in flour, oatmeal, and salt until crumbly. Press two-thirds mixture into dish. Reserve ⅓ to sprinkle over top. Spread date mixture evenly over crust. Sprinkle remaining crumbs evenly over top. Cook on HI 7 to 8 minutes, or until set, rotating dish if mixture is cooking unevenly. Cool before cutting.

Raisin-Nut Bars _____ 18 to 20 bars

Total Cooking Time: 11 to 13 minutes

1 **cup raisins, chopped**
½ **cup apple juice**
2 **tablespoons sugar**
1 **teaspoon all-purpose flour**
½ **cup chopped nuts, divided**
½ **cup butter or margarine, softened**
½ **cup firmly packed brown sugar**
1 **teaspoon vanilla**
1 **teaspoon baking powder**
¾ **cup all-purpose flour**
1½ **cups quick-cooking oats**

Combine raisins, apple juice, sugar, and the 1 teaspoon flour in 4-cup glass measure. Cover with plastic wrap. Cook on HI 3 to 4 minutes, or until thickened, stirring once during cooking time. Stir in ¼ cup of nuts; set aside.

Cream butter, brown sugar, and vanilla in mixing bowl. Mix baking powder with ¾ cup flour; add to creamed mixture. Stir in oats and remaining nuts. Press half of the flour mixture into 8-inch round microproof baking dish. Cook on HI 3 minutes, or until surface is no longer moist. Spread raisin mixture on top. Spoon remaining flour mixture over raisin filling; press lightly. Cook on HI 5 to 6 minutes, or until no longer moist on top. Let stand in pan on heat-resistant counter top or breadboard until cool. Cut into squares.

Brownies ———————————— 18 to 20 servings

Total Cooking Time: 6 to 7½ minutes

½ **cup butter or margarine**
2 **ounces unsweetened baking chocolate**
2 **eggs**
¾ **cup sugar**
½ **cup all-purpose flour**
1 **teaspoon baking powder**
1 **teaspoon vanilla**
¼ **teaspoon salt**
1 **cup chopped nuts**
   Confectioners sugar

Place butter and chocolate in 4-cup glass measure. Cook on HI 1 to 1½ minutes, or until butter is melted. (Chocolate will not appear melted until stirred.) Beat eggs in mixing bowl. Add sugar, flour, baking powder, vanilla, and salt; blend well. Stir into chocolate mixture. Stir in nuts. Pour into 9-inch square microproof baking dish. Cook on HI 5 to 6 minutes. (Brownies will be moist but will become firm as they cool). Sprinkle with confectioners sugar. Cool before cutting into squares.

Chocolate Chip Bars ———————— 2 dozen

Total Cooking Time: 8 to 9 minutes

½ **cup butter or margarine**
¾ **cup firmly packed brown sugar**
2 **eggs, lightly beaten**
1 **teaspoon vanilla**
½ **cup all-purpose flour**
1 **cup chopped nuts**
1 **cup semisweet chocolate chips**
1 **teaspoon baking powder**
   Confectioners sugar or instant cocoa drink mix

Place butter in 2-quart glass measure or microproof bowl. Cook on HI 1 minute, or until melted. Stir in brown sugar, eggs, and vanilla. Stir in remaining ingredients, except confectioners sugar. Spread in 9-inch square microproof baking dish. Cook on HI 7 to 8 minutes, rotating dish if mixture is cooking unevenly. Let stand in pan to cool. Sprinkle with confectioners sugar. Cut into squares.

Brownies, Chocolate Chip Bars,
Pecan Dream Bars (page 164),
Date-Orange Bars (page 165) ➔

Lemon Bars _____ 16 bars

Total Cooking Time: 9 to 10 minutes

1 **cup all-purpose flour**
½ **cup butter or margarine, softened**
⅓ **cup confectioners sugar**
2 **eggs**
1 **cup sugar**
2 **tablespoons all-purpose flour**
2 **tablespoons lemon juice**
1 **teaspoon grated lemon rind**
½ **teaspoon baking powder**
Confectioners sugar

Mix flour, butter, and ⅓ cup confectioners sugar until crumbly. Press into bottom of 9-inch square microproof baking dish. Cook on HI 4½ minutes. Combine remaining ingredients, except last addition of confectioners sugar; beat with electric mixer until smooth. Pour over baked crust. Cook on HI 4½ to 5½ minutes, or until center tests done, rotating dish if mixture is rising unevenly. Let stand, covered with waxed paper, 4 minutes. Remove waxed paper, cool, and cut into bars. Sprinkle with confectioners sugar.

Pineapple-Tapioca Mallow _____ 4 to 5 servings

Total Cooking Time: 6 to 7 minutes

1¾ **cups milk**
1 **can (8 ounces) pineapple chunks, drained, syrup reserved**
1 **package (3¼ ounces) tapioca pudding mix**
1 **tablespoon lemon juice**
½ **cup miniature marshmallows**
¼ **cup sliced maraschino cherries, drained**

Add pineapple syrup to milk to equal 2 cups. Combine pudding mix and milk mixture in 4-cup glass measure; stir to dissolve pudding. Cook on 70 for 6 to 7 minutes, or until mixture comes to a full boil, stirring every 2 minutes. Stir in lemon juice. Let stand 15 minutes. Stir in pineapple, marshmallows, and cherries; chill. Stir. Spoon into sherbet glasses to serve.

Chocolate Rum Sauce _____ 1 cup

Total Cooking Time: 1 minute

½ **cup (3 ounces) semisweet chocolate pieces**
2 **tablespoons light cream**
1 **cup miniature marshmallows**
1 **tablespoon rum**
¼ **teaspoon salt**
¼ **cup chopped nuts**

Combine chocolate, cream, and marshmallows in 2-cup glass measure. Cook on HI 1 minute, or until chocolate and marshmallows are melted. Stir to combine. Add rum, salt, and nuts. Serve warm over ice cream or cake.

Lemon Dessert Sauce _____ 1½ cups

Total Cooking Time: 4 minutes

1 cup water
½ cup sugar
1 tablespoon cornstarch
**2 tablespoons butter or
      margarine**
**2 teaspoons fresh lemon
      juice**
**½ teaspoon grated lemon
      rind**
Dash salt
	Combine water, sugar, and cornstarch in 4-cup glass measure. Stir to dissolve. Cook on HI 4 minutes, or until slightly thickened. Add butter, lemon juice, rind, and salt. Stir until butter is melted. Serve warm or cold over cake or pudding.

Raspberry Sauce _____ ¾ cup

Total Cooking Time: 6½ to 8½ minutes

1 package (10 ounces) frozen raspberries **2 teaspoons cornstarch** **1 teaspoon lemon juice**	Place frozen berries in 4-cup glass measure. Cook on 30 for 2½ to 3½ minutes, or until thawed. Drain juice, reserve. Combine cornstarch with 1 tablespoon of raspberry juice; mix to make a paste. Stir in remaining raspberry juice. Stir in berries. Cook on HI 4 to 5 minutes, stirring every 1 minute. Stir in lemon juice. Chill before serving. Serve over ice cream, cheesecake, pudding, or butter cake.

Cranberry-Orange Sauce _____ 2 cups

Total Cooking Time: 7 to 8 minutes

3 cups fresh cranberries **½ cup sugar** **⅓ cup water** **1 tablespoon grated orange peel** **⅓ cup fresh orange juice**	Combine cranberries, sugar, and water in 2-quart microproof bowl. Cover with plastic wrap. Cook on HI 6 to 7 minutes, or until berries pop. Stir in orange peel and juice. Cover. Cook on HI 1 minute. Let stand until cool. Cover and refrigerate until ready to serve.

INDEX

Acorn Squash with Peas.......... 72
Almond(s)
   Bark, Chocolate 162
   Green Beans and.............. 75
Appetizers 37-48
See also Dip(s)
   Reheating Guide, Convenience... 38
Apple Pie
   Crunchy 154
   Deep-Dish Apple and Cheese Pie 153
Asparagus
   Blanching Guide................ 71
   Casserole, Ham, Asparagus,
     and Noodle 95
   Cooking Guide 68
   with Mustard Sauce 76
Avocado Omelet................. 82
Bacon
   Cooking Guide 105
   Defrosting Guide 101
   Olive and Bacon Wraps 46
   Sandwich, Tomato, Cheese and .. 62
   Spinach and Bacon, Hot........ 75
   and Tomato Rabbit............. 63
Baked Ham Classic.............. 109
Baked Salmon Steaks............ 138
Banana Cake 155
Barbecued Chuck Roast 107
Basic White Sauce............... 77
Bass, Stuffed................... 139
Bean(s)
   Blanching Guide................ 71
   Cooking Guide 68
   Green Beans and Almonds 75
   Three Bean Bake 76
Beef......................... 99-109
See also Ground Beef; Roast(s); Steak(s)
   defrost 35
   Cooking Guide 102-103
   Defrosting Guide 101
   Reheating Guide, Convenience . 105
   Soup
     Beef Vegetable 58
     Onion-..................... 58
   Stew, Hearty Beef Vegetable 96
Beverages 42-48
   Cooking Guide, Hot Drinks....... 39
Blanching Guide, Vegetables 71
Blueberry Muffins................ 152
"Boiled" Dinner.................. 89
Braised Celery and Peas 74

Braised Lamb Shanks............ 114
Bread(s). *See also* Muffins; Rolls
   Cheese Bread, Savory 157
   Convenience Breads,
     Reheating Guide 145
   Corn Bread Ring, Honey 146
   Garlic 157
   Molasses Buttermilk........... 154
   Onion Herb 158
   Pineapple Zucchini 146
   Reheating Guide, Convenience . 145
   Stuffing...................... 126
Broccoli
   Blanching Guide................ 71
   Cooking Guide 68
   Soup, Cream of................ 60
   and Sour Cream 77
Brownies 166
   Reheating Guide 160
Brown & Serve Rolls 158
Brussels Sprouts
   Cooking Guide 68
   with Walnut Butter 80
Buttermilk Bread, Molasses 154
Butter Pecan Ice Cream Pie 153
Cabbage
   Cooking Guide 68
   Creamed 77
   Kielbasa and.................. 88
Cake(s)
   Banana...................... 155
   Cheesecake and
     Raspberry Sauce 149
   Chocolate Cherry Bundt........ 150
   Coconut Cake, Classic 155
   Cupcakes, Pumpkin........... 148
   Peanutty Chocolate 148
   Reheating Guide, Convenience . 160
Candied Yams................... 80
Candy
   Chocolate
     Almond Bark 162
     Raisin Nut Clusters 161
   Fairy Food 162
   Fudge
     Chocolate.................. 161
     Penuche.................. 161
   Peanut Brittle, Dry-Roasted 163
Cantonese Beef and Vegetables.... 96
Carrot(s)
   and Basil Bake 74

Blanching Guide............... 71
Cooking Guide 69
Casseroles...................... 87-98
Chicken and Rice.............. 95
Chicken and Spinach 97
cooking tips................ 26-27
defrosting..................... 88
Ham
Asparagus, and Noodle 95
Spaghetti 98
Potato and Onion 78
Quick Cassoulet 92
Shrimp Casserole, Sweet and Sour 90
Spanish Rice Supper............ 89
Tuna-Cashew................. 98
Cauliflower
Blanching Guide............... 71
Cooking Guide 69
au Gratin 80
Celery
Braised Celery and Peas 74
Cooking Guide 69
Cereal......................... 66
Cheddar
Baked Eggs.................... 85
Cheese Dip, Clam 47
Cheese
Bacon and Tomato Rabbit 63
Bread, Savory 157
Cheddar
Baked Eggs.................... 85
Cheese Dip, Clam 47
Chicken and Ham Roll-Ups,
Swiss........................ 122
Dip(s)
Clam Cheddar................. 47
Shrimp Cream................. 47
Tomato Jalapeño 44
Fondue 86
Frosting, Cream Cheese........ 156
Hot Dog Cheese Wrap 59
Macaroni and 93
Nacho Rounds 46
Noodles and 86
Pie, Deep-Dish Apple and 153
Sandwich, Tomato, Cheese
and Bacon 62
Soup, Hearty Cheese and Frank . 55
Swiss Chicken and Ham Roll-Ups 122
Tomato Jalapeño Cheese Dip 44
Tuna, Tomato, and 64
Welsh Rabbit on Toast........... 86
Cheeseburgers................... 63
Cheesecake. *See also* Cake(s)
and Raspberry Sauce 149
Reheating Guide 160
Cherry Bundt Cake, Chocolate 150
Chicken 115-27
defrost...................... 36
Breasts with Cashews.......... 124

Casserole
Chicken and Rice............. 95
Chicken and Spinach 97
Cooking Guide 118
Croissants 64
Defrosting Guide 117
Drumsticks Dinner, Wagonwheel. 125
and Ham Roll-Ups, Swiss....... 122
Hawaiian 125
Herb-Seasoned................ 127
Mandarin Chicken and Rice..... 122
Oven Baked 119
Quartered, auto defrost.......... 36
Reheating Guide, Convenience . 119
Soup, Lemon Chicken Rice 58
Steaks........................ 124
Stroganoff 120
Tetrazzini 120
Veronique.................... 121
Whole Chicken, Stuffed......... 126
Wings Canton 44
Chili
Eldorado..................... 52
Enchilada Chili Bake 92
Chocolate
Almond Bark 162
Bars, Chocolate Chip 166
Cake
Cherry Bundt................ 150
Peanutty.................... 148
Fairy Food 162
Fudge 161
Hot Chocolate Malt 48
Raisin Nut Clusters 161
Sauce, Chocolate Rum......... 168
Chowder. *See* Soup(s)
Cider, Spiced.................... 42
Clam(s)
Casino 141
Cooking Guide 132
with Creamy Garlic Sauce 142
Dip, Clam Cheddar Cheese...... 47
Classic Coconut Cake........... 155
Classic Omelet 83
Coffeecake, Reheating Guide 145
Cold Eggplant Appetizer 40
Cookies
Brownies 166
Chocolate Chip Bars 166
Date-Orange Bars 165
frozen, Reheating Guide........ 160
Lemon Bars................... 168
Pecan Dream Bars............. 164
Raisin-Nut Bars............... 165
Cooking Guide(s).
See also Reheating Guide(s)
Drinks, Hot................... 39
Eggs........................ 67
Fish and Shellfish............. 132
Meat 102-105

Poultry 118
Pudding and Pie Filling Mix 144
Rice 67
Soups 51
Vegetables 68-70
  Canned 71
Corn
  Blanching Guide 71
  Chowder, Seafood 52
  Cooking Guide 69
  in-the-Husk 76
  Scalloped 75
Corn Bread Ring, Honey 146
Corned beef
  "Boiled" Dinner 89
  Cooking Guide 103
Cornish Hens
  Cooking Guide 118
  Defrosting Guide 117
  Halved 121
Country Meatballs 106
Crab
  Cooking Guide 132
  Defrosting Guide 131
  Imperial 141
  Stuffed Mushrooms 39
Cranberry-Orange Sauce 169
Cream of Broccoli Soup 60
Cream Cheese
  Dip, Shrimp 47
  Frosting 156
Creamed Cabbage 77
Creamed Onions Williamsburg 72
Cream of Mushroom Soup 56
Creamy Garlic Sauce, Clams with . 142
Croissants, Chicken 64
Crunchy Apple Pie 154
Cucumber Sauce, Salmon
  Steak with 138
Cupcakes. *See also* Cake(s)
  Pumpkin 148
  Reheating Guide 160
custard, egg, Cooking Guide 144
Date-Orange Bars 165
Deep-Dish Apple and Cheese Pie . 153
Defrosting 29-36
See also Defrosting; Reheating
  Guide(s)
    Fish and Shellfish 131
    Meat 101
    Poultry 117
Denver Scramble 82
Desserts
See also Cake(s); Candy; Cookies;
  Dessert Sauce(s); Fruit; Pie(s)
  Reheating Guide, Convenience . 160
Dessert Sauce(s)
  Chocolate Rum Sauce 168
  Cranberry-Orange Sauce 169

Lemon 169
Raspberry Sauce 169
Dip(s)
  Clam Cheddar Cheese 47
  Liver Brandy Spread 40
  Shrimp Cream Cheese 47
  Tomato Jalapeño Cheese 44
Dry-Roasted Peanut Brittle 163
Duckling
  Cooking Guide 118
  Defrosting Guide 117
  Orange-Glazed 128
Eggplant
  Appetizer, Cold 40
  Cooking Guide 69
Egg(s). *See also* Omelet(s)
  Cheddar Baked 85
  Cooking Guide(s) 67
  Low-Cal Eggs Oriental 83
  Palace 85
  Scramble, Denver 82
  Sunny-Side-Up 83
Eldorado Chili 52
Enchilada Chili Bake 92
Exotic Lamb Ragout 114
Fairy Food 162
Fish 129-40
See also Shellfish
  Bass, Stuffed 139
  Chowder, Manhattan Seafood 56
  Cooking Guide 132
  Defrosting Guide 131
  Fillets
    Amandine 133
    defrost 35
    Herb-Crumbed 134
    Halibut and Vegetables 134
    Hawaiian Baked 139
    Poached 133
    Reheating Guide, Convenience . 132
  Salmon Steak(s)
    Baked 138
    with Cucumber Sauce 138
  Sole, Stuffed Fillet of,
    with Shrimp Sauce 136
  Tuna
    Cashew Casserole 98
    Mushroom Patties 135
    Tomato, and Cheese 64
    and Vegetable Pie 135
    Vegetable Soup 54
Fondue, Cheese 86
Frank Reuben 60
Frosting
  Cream Cheese 156
  White Cap Glaze 150
Fruit.
See also specific fruit
  frozen, Reheating Guide 160

Salad, Pantry. 163
Fudge
   Chocolate. 161
   Penuche. 161
Garlic Bread 157
Glazed Turkey Legs. 128
Glaze, White Cap 150
Green Beans
   and Almonds. 75
   Blanching Guide. 71
   Cooking Guide 68
   Three Bean Bake 76
Ground Beef.
See also Meatball(s); Meat Loaf
   defrost. 35
   Beefburger Stroganoff. 90
   Cheeseburgers. 63
   Chili, Eldorado. 52
   Cooking Guide 102
   Defrosting Guide 101
   Enchilada Chili Bake 92
   Gumbo 89
   Muffin Toppers, Beef 39
   Quick Cassoulet 92
   Soup, Beef Vegetable 58
   Spanish Rice Supper. 89
   Stuffed Mushrooms, Mexican. 42
   Stuffed Peppers, Spicy 107
   Supper Pie. 93
   Tacos and Fixin's, Beef 59
Halibut and Vegetables. 134
Halved Cornish Hens 121
Ham. *See also* Pork
   Baked Ham Classic 109
   Casserole
      Asparagus, and Noodle 95
      Spaghetti 98
   Cooking Guide 104
   and Potato Scallop. 97
   Steak, Smothered. 112
   Swiss Chicken, and Ham Roll-Ups 122
Hamburger(s)
   Cheeseburgers. 63
   Cooking Guide 102
Hashed Brown Potato Bake 79
Hawaiian Baked Fish. 139
Hawaiian Chicken 125
Hearty Beef Vegetable Stew 96
Hearty Cheese and Frank Soup 55
Herb
   Bread, Onion. 158
   Crumbed Fish Fillets 134
   Seasoned Chicken. 127
Homemade Pie Shell. 156
Honey Corn Bread Ring 146
Honey-Glazed Pork Roast 110
Horseradish-Onion Beef Roast 108
Hot Buttered Lemonade 42
Hot Chocolate Malt 48

Hot Dog(s)
   Cheese Wrap 59
   Cooking Guide 105
   Defrosting Guide 101
   Frank Reuben 60
   Soup, Hearty Cheese and Frank . 55
Hot Spinach and Bacon 75
Ice Cream Pie, Butter Pecan 153
Jalapeño Cheese Dip, Tomato. 44
Kielbasa and Cabbage. 88
Lamb
   defrost. 36
   Cooking Guide 103-104
   Defrosting Guide 101
   Ragout, Exotic. 114
   Shanks, Braised 114
Leftover Meat Stew 109
Lemon
   Bars. 168
   Dessert Sauce 169
   Soup, Lemon Chicken Rice 58
Lentil Soup. 53
Liver
   Brandy Spread 40
   Defrosting Guide 101
Lobster tails
   Cooking Guide 132
   Defrosting Guide 131
Low-Cal Eggs Oriental 83
Macaroni and Cheese. 93
Mandarin Chicken and Rice. 122
Manhattan Seafood Chowder 56
Meat 99-114
See also Beef; Lamb; Pork; Veal
   Cooking Guides 102-105
   Defrosting Guide 101
   Reheating Guide,
      Convenience Beef 105
   spread, canned, Reheating Guide 38
   Stew, Leftover 109
Meatball(s)
   Country. 106
   Polynesian 43
   Soup 53
Meat Loaf
   Cooking Guide 102
   Super Meat Loaf Ring 106
Mexican Stuffed Mushrooms 42
Minestrone, Quick 55
Molasses Buttermilk Bread. 154
Muffin(s)
   Beef Muffin Toppers. 39
   Blueberry 152
   Raisin-Oatmeal 152
   Reheating Guide 145
Mushroom(s)
   Cooking Guide 69
   Crab-Stuffed 39
   Mexican Stuffed 42

Patties, Tuna- 135
Soup, Cream of. 56
Nacho Rounds 46
Nibblers Bowl 43
Noodle(s)
Casserole, Ham, Asparagus, and 95
and Cheese. 86
Nut(s)
Bars, Raisin- 165
Clusters, Chocolate-Raisin 161
Nibblers Bowl 43
Oatmeal Muffins, Raisin-. 152
Olive and Bacon Wraps 46
Omelet(s). See also Egg(s)
Avocado. 82
Classic 83
Onion(s)
Beef Soup 58
Blanching Guide. 71
Bread, Onion Herb. 158
Casserole, Potato and 78
Cooking Guide 69
Creamed Onions Williamsburg . . . 72
Pie in Rice Crust. 79
Orange
Bars, Date 165
Glazed Duckling. 128
Sauce, Cranberry-. 169
Oven Baked Chicken 119
Oysters
Cooking Guide 132
Defrosting Guide 131
Palace Eggs 85
Pantry Fruit Salad. 163
Parslied Potatoes 78
Parsnips
Blanching Guide. 71
Cooking Guide 69
Pasta
Beefburger Stroganoff. 90
Macaroni and Cheese. 93
Noodle(s)
Casserole, Ham, Asparagus, and 95
and Cheese. 86
reheating 66
Spaghetti Casserole, Ham 98
Supper Pie. 93
Peanut Brittle, Dry-Roasted 163
Peanutty Chocolate Cake. 148
Pears, Poached 164
Peas
Acorn Squash with. 72
Blanching Guide. 71
Braised Celery and 74
Cooking Guide 69
Pecan
Butter Pecan Ice Cream Pie 153
Dream Bars 164
Rum Pie 149

Penuche Fudge 161
Peppers, Spicy Stuffed 107
Pie(s). See also Pie Shell(s)
Apple
Crunchy 154
Deep-Dish Apple and Cheese 153
Ice Cream Pie, Butter Pecan 153
Onion Pie in Rice Crust. 79
Pecan Rum 149
Reheating Guide, Convenience . 160
Supper 93
Tuna and Vegetable. 135
Pie Shell(s)
Homemade 156
Rice Pie Crust. 156
Pineapple-Tapioca Mallow 168
Pineapple Zucchini Bread 146
Pizza
Reheating Guide, Convenience. . . 38
Topper 48
Poached Eggs, Cooking Guide. 67
Poached Fish 133
Poached Pears 164
Polynesian Meatballs 43
Pork. See also Bacon; Ham; Sausage
Chops
defrost. 35
Sauced. 112
Cooking Guide 104
Defrosting Guide 101
Ribs with Dill and Tomato. 110
Roast, Honey-Glazed 110
Potato(es)
Casserole, Potato and Onion. 78
Cooking Guide 70
au Gratin 78
Ham and Potato Scallop 97
Hashed Brown Potato Bake 79
mashed, reheating 66
Parslied. 78
Reheating Guide, Convenience. . . 70
Poultry. 115-28
See also Chicken; Cornish Hens;
Duckling; Turkey
Cooking Guide 118
Defrosting Guide 117
Reheating Guide, Convenience . 119
Pudding
and Pie Filling Mix, Cooking Guide 144
Pineapple-Tapioca Mallow 168
Pumpkin Cupcakes 148
Quartered Chicken, auto defrost. . . . 36
Quick Cassoulet 92
Quick Minestrone 55
Raisin(s)
Nut Bars. 165
Nut Clusters, Chocolate 161
Oatmeal Muffins 152

Raspberry Sauce 169
  Cheesecake and 149
Reheating Guide(s)
  Appetizers, Convenience 38
  Beef, Convenience. 105
  Breads, Convenience 145
  Poultry, Convenience. 119
  Seafood, Convenience 132
  Vegetables, Convenience. 70
Ribs. *See* Spareribs
Rice
  Casserole, Chicken and 95
  Cooking Guide 67
  Mandarin Chicken and 122
  Pie Crust 156
    Onion Pie in. 79
  reheating 66
  Soup, Lemon Chicken. 58
  Spanish Rice Supper. 89
Roast(s)
  Beef Roast, Horseradish-Onion. . 108
  Chuck Roast, Barbecued 107
  Cooking Guide 102-104
  Defrosting Guide 101
  Pork Roast, Honey-Glazed 110
Rolled Rib Roast, defrost 35
Rolls. *See* Bread(s)
Salmon Steak(s)
  Baked. 138
  with Cucumber Sauce. 138
Sandwich(es).
See also Hamburger(s); Hot Dog(s)
  Bacon and Tomato Rabbit 63
  Barbecued Chuck Roast
    (variation). 107
  Chicken Croissants 64
  Pizza Topper 48
  Super 62
  Tomato, Cheese and Bacon. 62
  Tuna, Tomato, and Cheese. 64
Sauced Pork Chops. 112
Sauce(s). *See also* Dessert Sauce(s)
  Cucumber, Salmon Steak with. . , 138
  Garlic Sauce, Creamy, Clams
with 142
  Mustard, Asparagus with 76
  Shrimp, Stuffed Fillet of Sole with 136
  White Sauce, Basic 77
Sausage(s)
  Reheating Guide, canned. 38
  Cooking Guide 104-105
  Defrosting Guide 101
  Kielbasa and Cabbage. 88
Savory Cheese Bread 157
Scalloped Corn. 75
Scallops
  Cooking Guide 132
  Defrosting Guide 131
Scampi. 142

Scrambled Eggs, Cooking Guide . . . 67
Seafood 129-42
See also Fish; Shellfish
  Chowder
    Manhattan 56
    Seafood Corn 52
  Cooking Guide 132
  Defrosting Guide 131
  Reheating Guide, Convenience . 132
Shellfish. *See also* Fish; Shrimp
  Chowder
    Manhattan Seafood 56
    Seafood Corn 52
  Clams Casino 141
  Clams with Creamy Garlic Sauce 142
  Cooking Guide 132
  Crab Imperial 141
  Defrosting Guide 131
  Reheating Guide, Convenience
  Seafood 132
Shrimp
  defrost. 35
  Casserole, Sweet and Sour 90
  Chowder, Seafood Corn 52
  Cooking Guide 132
  Defrosting Guide 131
  Dip, Shrimp Cream Cheese 47
  Reheating Guide, Convenience . 132
  Sauce, Stuffed Fillet of Sole with 136
  Scampi. 142
Smothered Ham Steak 112
Sole, Stuffed Fillet of,
  with Shrimp Sauce. 136
Soup
  Beef Vegetable 58
  Cheese and Frank Soup, Hearty . 55
  Cream of Broccoli 60
  Cream of Mushroom 56
  Lemon Chicken Rice 58
  Lentil 53
  Meatball 53
  Minestrone, Quick 55
  Onion-Beef. 58
  Seafood
    Corn Chowder. 52
    Manhattan Seafood Chowder . . 56
  Tuna-Vegetable. 54
  Turkey. 54
Spanish Rice Supper. 89
Spareribs
  Cooking Guide 104
  Defrosting Guide 101
  Ribs with Dill and Tomato 110
Spiced Cider 42
Spicy Stuffed Peppers 107
Spinach
  and Bacon, Hot. 75
  Blanching Guide. 71
  Casserole, Chicken and 97

176

Cooking Guide 70
Squash
    Acorn Squash with Peas 72
    Cooking Guide 70
Steak(s)
    Cantonese Beef and Vegetables . 96
    Cooking Guide 103
    Defrosting Guide 101
    Ham Steak, Smothered 112
Stew(s)
    Beef Vegetable Stew, Hearty 96
    Lamb Ragout, Exotic 114
    Meat Stew, Leftover 109
    Veal-Caraway 113
Stuffed Bass 139
Stuffed Fillet of Sole
    with Shrimp Sauce 136
Stuffed Peppers, Spicy 107
Stuffed Whole Chicken 126
Stuffing, Bread 126
Super Meat Loaf Ring 106
Super Sandwich 62
Supper Pie 93
Sweet Cardamom Rolls 150
Sweet potatoes, Cooking Guide 69
    Candied Yams 80
Sweet and Sour Shrimp Casserole . . 90
Swiss Chicken and Ham Roll-Ups . 122
Tacos
    and Fixin's, Beef 59
    mini, Reheating Guide 38
Tapioca
    Cooking Guide 144
    Mallow, Pineapple- 168
Three Bean Bake 76
Tomato(es)
    Bacon and Tomato Rabbit 63
    Dip, Tomato Jalapeño Cheese . . . 44
    Sandwich, Tomato, Cheese
        and Bacon 62
    Tuna, Tomato, and Cheese 64
Tuna
    Casserole
        Reheating Guide, Convenience 132
        Cashew 98
    Patties, Tuna-Mushroom 135

Pie, Tuna and Vegetable 135
Soup, Tuna-Vegetable 54
Tomato, and Cheese 64
Turkey
    Cooking Guide 118
    Crunch 127
    Defrosting Guide 117
    Legs, Glazed 128
    Reheating Guide, Convenience . 119
    Soup 54
Turnips
    Blanching Guide 71
    Cooking Guide 70
Veal
    Cooking Guide 104
    Defrosting Guide 101
    Parmigiana 113
    Stew, Veal-Caraway 113
Vegetable(s).
See also specific vegetable
    Blanching Guide 71
    Canned, Cooking Guide 71
    Cantonese Beef and 96
    Convenience, Reheating Guide . . . 70
    Cooking Guide 68-70
    Halibut and 134
    Pie, Tuna and 135
    Reheating Guide, Convenience . . . 70
    Soup
        Beef Vegetable 58
        Minestrone, Quick 55
        Tuna-Vegetable 54
    Stew, Hearty Beef 96
Wagonwheel Drumsticks Dinner . . . 125
Walnut Butter, Brussels Sprouts with 80
Welsh Rabbit on Toast 86
White Cap Glaze 150
White Sauce, Basic 77
Wine Warmer 47
Yams, Candied 80
Zucchini
    Blanching Guide 71
    Bread, Pineapple 146
    Cooking Guide 70
    Provençale 74